LETTERS FROM THE LOONEY BIN

THATCHER C NALLEY

Foreword

A mental institution for family members of great wealth, the Emerson Rose Asylum opened its doors in the summer of 1952. In the late 1970s, the asylum became completely abandoned - all patients, doctors, and staff completely vanished and were never seen again. The events circling this mass exodus have been one of the most baffling disappearances in history...until now. Upon the demolition of the Emerson building, a stack of letters was found hidden inside an asylum mattress. These letters were addressed to the pseudonym, Dr. Quill, and written by the patients as they documented the final days of the Emerson Rose Asylum. The names have been changed, but the stories have not. Though their identities are protected, the essence of these patients' challenges, triumphs, corruption, salvation and, most of all, their human spirit, has been untouched. Their journey will become your journey as each patient re-tells their personal story in these, Letters from the Looney Bin.

DOCTOR'S NOTE

September 13, 1978

I do pray these letters land in the hands of good valor. For, if on the contrary, then the secrets which seep through these walls will be forever sealed. I would have favored the allocation of more time; however, recent events have not afforded me such luxury. This annotation will be minimal; however, I feel the enclosed letters tell the story more than I could ever herald.

I find it admirable that the patients truly believe they will be victorious, though I'm afraid when this mutiny concludes, they will completely perish. The chain of events has prematurely set in motion that which cannot be undone.

My own fate is of great uncertainty. If it comes to be that I am not a causality of this war, then there is a probability of great measure that the enclosed letters will leave these walls. From there it would be most desirous…

Oh, dear Lord, I must immediately bring this note to a close, for I can hear through my door that the battle has ensued and has…oh, dear Lord…Lord, help us!

Godspeed!

Dr. Quill

THE LETTERS

1

SCREAMING MAD

11 months prior

October 29, 1977

Hi, Dr. Quill, my name is Sabel and I scream. I scream a lot. They hate it here when I scream. So they, the whiteys, lock me in my room to scream so they don't have to listen. I scream and scream until blood spurts from my mouth. Then I like to put my fingers in the blood and use it as red paint to wipe all over their precious padded, white walls. That always makes me laugh. Laugh really loud. Well, until a nurse comes and pokes me with a needle. Then the laughing stops. I think the whiteys like it when I get a needle because the last thing I see before my eyes flicker shut, are white coats and big clown smiles leaning over me.

I hate all the whiteys here and mess with them whenever I can. Like at meal times. I wait until none of them are looking then duck underneath one of the long metal food tables. Once I'm comfortably crouched and out of sight, I let out a blood-curdling scream. The whiteys scurry like rats looking for cheese to find me. Then, just as one of them spots me, I stop screaming, pull back my long black hair, reveal my blue-eyed squinting glare and give them a hard grin. The new whiteys get mad and stomp off. It's funny. The old whiteys just drag me out from under the table and get a nurse to stick me with a needle. I don't think that's funny.

There are also the crazies. They are not as annoying as the whiteys, but I mess with them, too. Sometimes, in the middle of the night after my needle stuff wears off, I sit up and throw my head back and let out a piercing screech. The crazies bang on their walls and yell at me to shut up. So I stop, and laugh. Then I wait long enough for them to fall back to sleep and I begin to scream and screech even louder. None of the crazies here like me, but I don't care; they're just a bunch of whackies anyway.

I have been here for over ten years. That's because, when I was five, a doctor told Momma that nothing would stop my screaming. He said it would be better if I were sent away. Momma wept all night. The next day, Momma told me she had used a needle when I was in her tummy and that was how my brain became broken. That is why I scream. I don't understand because, here, when they put a needle in me, it stops the screaming. Momma said she used the kind of needle that was hurtful. One day when she came to visit, I told Momma she should try the needles here cause they make the hurt go away. She laughed then cried. That made me scream. The whiteys drug me away. I watched Momma reach for me with tears as I kicked and screamed for them to let me go. That was the last time Momma came to see me.

Even though Momma doesn't visit anymore, she sends me letters on pretty paper with lots of hearts. Sometimes, I get these bad headaches though, and then I can't read them very well, so I make up her words. They only let me read the letter once then I have to give it back them. The whiteys tell me the letters are being kept in a safe place for now but a letter has not come for a very long time. Momma must be really busy. I sent her a picture that I drew of me not screaming, but it was sent back. The whiteys told me the envelope said Momma didn't live there anymore. That mailman is wrong, though, because I know where my Momma lives. A few years ago, I used to visit Momma at her place on the weekends sometimes. That was fun. We would play games and watch TV together. My favorite show was

Captain Kangaroo. Momma liked *I Love Lucy*, but that red-haired lady really got on my nerves. She had such a whiny voice; I wanted to tell her to shut up! But Momma liked her, so I pretended to like it, too.

Then Momma got this boyfriend. I didn't like him much. He was always mad or sleeping on the couch. He smelled funny in the mornings, too. I asked Momma what his strange smell was, and she said it was called whiskey. This is weird because when I get mad and wake up, I don't smell like whiskey.

I don't remember that boyfriend's name; I don't want to. He was always yelling at Momma, me, the television, the chair. . . . That guy yelled way more than I ever screamed. He should be in here with these crazies, not me. Anyway, that boyfriend didn't like my screaming, so I couldn't go see Momma anymore. She told me it was better that way, so I wouldn't see her get bruises cause that made me scream. Momma said she didn't want me to get bruises either.

I miss Momma a lot. I think about her all the time. I have tried, before, to stop screaming for her so we could live together again. I took the medicines, did the things they told me to rest my mind, but the whiteys always find a way to make me scream. Once, I went three whole months without screaming. Momma was so proud that she bought me a pink, stuffed unicorn. I named it "Hush-Hush" and kept it next to my sleeping pillow. Then, one night, I went into my room and found my unicorn on the floor with its head torn off. I screamed so hard that it took six whiteys and three needles to make me stop. After that, I decided it would be best just to let myself scream. It was too hard to make myself stop.

Dr. Huxley wouldn't have let them do that. He would have made them whiteys leave forever. Momma always came to see me when Dr. Huxley was here. He let me keep anything she gave me. It was good then. But he's dead now. And then these other whiteys came and they're meaner than Momma's boyfriend is. So I need to leave and

I will get to leave soon! This new doc here says he can really help me. The crazies say not to trust this new doc, but what do crazies know?

The new doc told me he would fix my throat so I will never scream again. He's not nice like Dr. Huxley, but he's not stupid like the whiteys. Anyway, I'm just excited because once the doctor fixes me, I'm gonna call and tell Momma! Then she won't have to be sad anymore and I can move back with her. The first thing I'm gonna ask Momma to do for sure, is paint my room all pink; I don't want any white walls!

Anyway, I can't remember this new doc's name, but he seemed really nice when I met him. He's not one of those talking doctors that are always asking you stupid questions about your mom and your dad. He's the kind of doctor that fixes broken parts on people. When I see him again, I'm gonna ask him his name cause when I get home I'm gonna get a kitten and name it after this doc. I hope his name isn't something stupid like Henry.

The annoying part of this has been the crazies. They keep telling me to stay away from this doc. That's just because "Smackie-Jackie" went to go see this doc a few weeks ago. She was really bad off. She is always hitting everyone, and not just slaps or little punches. She likes to clinch her hand into real tight fists then walk over to someone and start pounding on them as hard as she can. She is strong, too. She hit me once and I broke out into an uncontrollable screaming spasm. It freaked her out so bad that she took off running. She still won't come near me.

So this doc was supposed to do something so her arms wouldn't hit anymore, but I guess he had to cut off one of her arms instead. The whiteys told me the doc had to because there was a horrible infection in her arm caused by all the hitting she had done. The infection could have spread all over her body and killed her, so, really, this doc saved her life.

"Smackie-Jackie" doesn't seem to feel that way about it, though. She mostly crouches in a corner and cries. When she heard I was going in to see this doc, she told one of the crazies to tell me not to go. She told the crazy to tell me this new doc is a monster. I told the crazy I felt "Smackie-Jackie" was a little ungrateful snot. That this doc saved her life, and he's the kind I want to help me. The crazy walked off mumbling something about me being stupid or something, but I don't care.

Anyway, tomorrow is the big day. I told all the crazies how I would miss them once I moved back to Momma's. I won't really miss them though; I just wanted them to know I was going home. I already have all my stuff packed up. I also told one of the whiteys to call Momma and let her know I'm coming home. The whitey just nodded with a strange smile and then coughed a laugh. Sometimes I swear these whiteys are weirder than the crazies are. I don't care, though, because things are going to be all better after tomorrow. I can't wait to see Momma and her smile and give her a great big hug and tell her I love her. It's going to be the best day ever!

Well, Doc, I always did like you. When you would let us draw pictures and write letters during circle time, I liked that. I will write to you when I am home, if you don't mind. I need to go for now. I need to get some sleep so I can be well rested for the big day. Don't let these crazies drive you crazy!

November 29, 1977

It has been one month now, Dr. Quill, since that doctor fixed my throat. The whiteys always mock me whenever I walk by. They stare at me with their condescending smiles and then cup their hands around their ears, pretending like they are trying to hear my silent screams. I cry a lot, but no one can hear me. No one can hear me at all. For that doctor altered my throat to where I cannot make any sounds, no sounds at all. They allowed this to happen to me, those white coats. So now, when I see any of them, I smile quite sweetly. But once they are within range, I give them a solid fisted blow to the stomach, which always removes the goddamn smirks off their faces.

Yesterday, I dutifully promised with pleading eyes and a humble nod that I would not strike anyone anymore. Then, right as the isolation door opened, I darted out and dashed behind the nurses' station. I yanked a typewriter off the desk, ran up behind a white coat that was sitting down and then smashed the top of her head with the typewriter. Her body dropped to the floor and blood pooled all around my feet. At first, I thought it had looked like thick, dark cherry juice. The kind that can be poured out of a can to make pie, like my Momma use to make. I dropped the typewriter, squatted, and took a deep sniff of the puddle around my feet. The smell made me half cough - it was nothing like cherries for a pie and I leaned slightly forward, dipped my finger gently into the blood and wrote *Momma*.

Suddenly, the whiteys were grabbing and pushing and then shoving me to the ground. I lay on my stomach, unable to move, crushed by their weight. It hurt. They turned me over and pinned my hands, legs, and head to the cold hard floor. My eyes slowly met each of theirs as I lay there with a wide grin and they all knew I was laughing.

I don't know if that white shirt died. I don't care if she did. It made me feel better to watch her lie there like a deflated rubber doll and watch her bleached blonde hair turn a mud thick, reddish-brown.

The white coats truly despise me now, but they let this happen. Do know - I will turn all of their white shirts red. Including that doctor Victor Vanodin. They have only begun to witness the hell I am about to unleash.

As for now, though, I must bid farewell. I have much

planning to do and time is of the essence. My name is Sabella Clarice Silva and, no, I do not scream out loud any more… but on the inside, the screaming never stops.

2

THE EVE LULL

December 24, 1977

Oh Dearest Dr. Quill,

It was most important that I compose this letter to you now; for I cannot endure the anticipation much more. I cannot wait one more second in false hopes that he will suddenly step through that door. I have waited so long now. Days have turned into months, months into years, and yet he has not shown. Where is he? The thought of him never showing is maddening. He knows of everything! Would he not know my need of his presence through that door tonight!

The snow is falling again, this year. The ground is as white as these walls. I see the flurry of snow is growing thicker. Is that what is stopping him? I must tell you that this is what they, these new ones, tell me every single year. They tell me that the weather has forestalled him from arriving. Many times, I have believed them but I do not believe that is the reason at all. Where is he? For I have been so good. I really have. Except for that one occurrence when I bit a piece of the nurse's ear off. I must say, though, that nasty woman deserved such a demise. I did not need that shot. It was most unjust. So I do believe the red man will not hold that against me.

But then where is he? I have always wondered if he really wears all red, I wager he really wears black. Ha! Would that not be the discovery of the century? Hold on,

15

there is a noise. It is footsteps! They are heavy steps that are getting louder, louder…could it be him? Balderdash, no! I know those sinister steps, and they are not the steps of the red man. I know those steps. It's that orderly who is always trying to walk inversely so he can deceive me, but I know it is him. Bastard asshole. My body may be thin and frail, but this brain inside my balding skull is a strength beyond his simple comprehension.

The steps have now stopped at Millie's door, figures, and little whore. She would give it up to the Easter Bunny if she thought it would get her a bigger Easter basket. Ha! I have known walls smarter than that dumb broad.

I have digressed. Where is he? Where is the red man? Maybe it is too early. It is not past midnight. I had not thought of that! What was I thinking? He would never come the night before. I must, I shall, wait a couple hours. I can wait an hour. I do not want to fall asleep and miss his presence though. I will need to think of something to keep me awake. I know I could think of what I will say when he arrives. I haven't really decided much about that yet. What will I ask him? What would he know? He knows a lot about others, although the only thing I would want to know would be about all the bad stuff that others are doing. Like is that doctor banging Millie? Hell, everyone is banging Millie, so that is nothing to know. I wonder what he would know about that freaky guy with no legs who sings that same song repeatedly – "On top of old soakey". Moron. We all know it's "On top of ole no-key"….or what's more likely around here - on top of ole Millie. I suppose there is nothing really to ask of the man in red - I really only want my bike, as I have every year, my beautiful red bicycle.

Oh, Dr. Quill, I suppose my needs, my concerns of him arriving are really nothing of great matter to you or any other. I must tell you, though, that I have never written before, because I did not want my words or my thoughts to be used against me. They have before you know. They do that here.

Yet I must write you now, for I believe that my chance to write at all will soon be gone. As you know, the girl with one arm is making plans with all others who will join her to escape this hell. I do not know if I will join them. I suppose I could if I must. It did make me wonder, though, if you will abdicate the plan to escape. Will you go with us, Dr. Quill? I know I should, but I do not know if I will.

The girl with one arm says I could be so helpful. She knows I am sneaky. She knows that I know the layout of this place… step by step, inch by inch. It's true you know; I do know these things. I have been here the longest, one of the first to come to Emerson, you know. I have seen every nook and cranny in this establishment, though I am not familiar with the portion of the building Dr. V added. The place where they take others and do things. Awful things. Bastard assholes. But I know enough to be helpful, yes, yes, I could, but I do not know if I will.

Oh, where is he? Why has he not arrived? How will he…never mind, I forgot it has not been an hour yet. I wonder if he will bring what I asked. I have not ridden a bike since I was ten years of age. I have not done anything since then, but sit here waiting. Why is the man in red not here now? I do not want to wait anymore! I cannot wait another minute. Where is that man? Maybe he will not come. Balderdash, I say! Balderdash! For he will come, he will. I must be patient – a patient *patient*. Ha! For he will be here and he will bring me my bicycle and I will get out of here tonight. Yes, yes.

However, Dr. Quill, this time I will ride my bike so fast they will not catch me. No, no. Not like those bastard assholes did when I was ten. Yanking me off my red Mead bicycle. I told them my hands where bloody from falling down, but noooo, they did not believe me. They had to believe that little bitch who said I stabbed our father to death. Little whore! I hated him, that father, bastard asshole, bastard asshole, bastard asshole. I still do hate that man, but she did not. She tried to stop me, my sister Millie, but in the end, it looked like she helped me with stabbing him. That is what I told them in my confession. That is what the little tattle-telling slut gets.

Of course, they had to send Millie and me here together. They could not have the truth come out about the state Governor. I made it very clear why Millie and I off'd the good ole Governor. They tried to get me to change my story, but I would not. They sent us to a local looney bin at first. They did not want to discredit my father's name and they had hoped that they could get me "better" so they told the town that Millie and I had witnessed the murder of our father. I would not let such a story be told and let them know that I would tell everyone the truth. Yes, yes. I told them all about the bastard asshole. Word started seeping out, questions were being asked, and then Millie tried to kill herself while in the local looney bin, so they quickly shipped us here to Emerson. Where we have been ever since.

Dr. Huxley raised us like his own children, really. He did not hurt us. He even let my sister and I have our rooms next door to each other. Things were good then. Until that pasty skinned, red haired, Napoleon troll of an evil man Dr. Van Bastard Asshole showed up with his tormentors. Evil, evil I do tell you! This man would make Satan pray for benevolence. I hate him.

Oh, where is he? Is it midnight yet? How would I even know? Balderdash, I am not waiting anymore for him! Hold on. What is that noise? I hear jingling. Could it be? There is more jingling and, oh, there is laughing – bastard asshole, it is a laugh I know. It is that orderly again, who was banging my sister. He thinks he is so funny shaking his keys to sound like bells and getting my hopes up. He will not think it is funny when I run him over with my bicycle, now will he?

I dream often of when that day comes – I will start at the end of the hall and go full speed ahead, and knock him down. Then I will stop, get off my bike, walk over, and kick him. Kick! Kick! Kick! I will proudly announce, "Merry Christmas!" Then get back on my bicycle and ride out of here forever. Oh, how that thought makes me smile.

No, no, I cannot do that; I cannot kick that bad man. For that would make me a bad man and then the man in red would never come. Then I would never be able to get out of here. Bad thoughts, go away! No, no, I cannot have these thoughts. I must think nice thoughts. For I must get out of this looney bin and…and... What am I going to do when I am out of here? Definitely get some candy! And a goldfish. I miss my goldfish, Andy. He was always there for me. Until he died. He tasted funny going down.

Oh, where is he? I cannot do this anymore. I cannot wait in false hope that the red man will walk through that door. I…I…I wonder what present Millie got me this year? She always makes me a picture of a goldfish. I cannot wait until tomorrow when she sees the present I made for her. I drew a real pretty picture of a pink lily flower and I named the drawing "Mil-Lily". I think she will like that. She always likes my presents.

I remember the happiest time the man in red came. I was eight and Mille was six years of age. I had bought her the most pretty baby doll. It had long blonde hair, freckles, blue eyes, and a pink dress. It looked like Millie, which is why I had chosen it. She smiled so big at my presents. We always did good, real good that time of the year. Mother would decorate every nook and cranny of the house in celebration. Even when she had black and blue eyes, our house was filled with red and green. Best of all, though, about that day of gift opening, was that it was the one and only day our father did not drink.

"Out of respect of the Lord's birthday," Our father would jest, "I will not drink today – for Christ's sake!" He would laugh, mother would not.

Once a year we escaped his drunken wrath. With his

dark hair and dark eyes, father seemed an eight-foot tower of a man. Everyone became silent when he entered a room. He dressed in crisp suits and shiny crocodile shoes. On the day of gift opening, he seemed smaller, his voice not so deep and harsh; his face not so blue, cold. He actually smiled that year when I came down the stairs in my red and white stripped pajamas and found the red bike next to the tree. It had big letters on the tag that read "To: Wallie." I loved that bike so much. Mostly because I could ride away from father. It was the best gift ever. That left Millie there with him alone… but she should have asked for a bike, too.

The sun will almost be here and I cannot wait for the red man anymore. Maybe he doesn't visit looney bins, maybe I am wasting my time. This saddens me so.

Maybe he or it is them, yes, Dr. Quill, that is it! The evil tormentors keep the red man out! Why did I not think of this before? For the man in red always came when Dr. Huxley was alive. The man in red always left a gift with my name on it, never a bike, but I had not asked for a bike back then. I did not want to leave when Dr. Huxley was here. Now that THEY are here and those evil tormentors know I wait for the man in red, they also know that he would help me… so they keep him out. Yes, yes! They lock all the doors and have all the night guards keeping watch. It all makes sense now. They will not let him in here!

Then…that means I will never see the red man. I will never have my bicycle. That means I will be stuck here forever. I…I cannot be here forever. No, no! I must get out. I must leave and go where the red man can find me. I will tell Millie. I will tell her what I know. For she has the trust of the guards with the keys at night. She could get the keys and I know ways to escape.

We can do this. Yes, yes! Millie will help. She has to help me. She owes me that.

We will help that one arm lady and the others for I too

must leave out of here. It will be an ugly battle, but watching these bastard assholes perish at our hands will be pretty. Very pretty. The tormentors will be tormented – yes, yes, ha, ha, YES!

Yours Sincerely, etc.

Walter C. Hollum, Jr.

3

LOCO MOTIVE

January 13, 1978

Dear Dr. Quill,

The first time I tried to take my life I was in grade school. I remember clearly standing in the middle of the railroad tracks, waiting for the big black locomotive to come. The morning dew had formed gently on the long track of rails that surrounded me like a hug. I stood with my feet shoulder-width apart, hands on my hips. I was wearing my mother's white ruffled dress with bright pink flowers. It had been in mother's closet ever since she had received it from nana as a gift just a couple years prior. I felt mother would rather I chose a dress she despised.

The wait for the train had seemed to take forever as I methodically counted the paralleling wooden tracks for as far as I could see and then back again. I had done this at least a dozen times before the train finally started to make its way around the bend. The tall pines camouflaged the big engine at first, but I could see the smoke above the tree tops moving closer and closer. My heart pounded inside my chest and I smiled. She was coming for me and I smiled excitedly, waiting!

"Darling, get off those tracks!" A man's voice yelled loudly from behind me. I ignored his warning and could hear his footsteps beginning to move faster.

"Did you hear me, little girl?" His voice becoming anxious, though elderly and cracked,

"Get down from there!" he ordered angrily.

Undeterred, I began counting the wooden beams out loud. "Nine, ten, eleven!"

The ole coot yelled at me again, but louder, quicker. I continued counting, louder, quicker. My toes in mother's pink heels now began to vibrate more and more. My eyes fixated on the bend that the fast approaching locomotive would come around, for I had wanted to meet the lady eye to eye.

The old man began screaming, "Move! Move!" And I could hear his feet stumble in the gravel as he ran towards me.

I continued to stand stringent and tall as I watched for the roaring engine and finally she came out from around the bend. Her bright lights forced me to close my eyes so that I had to squint, making it hard to stare into her face. I glanced up. The smoke coming from the top of her head looked like a long, billowing ponytail. The conductor must have noticed me at that point as the screeching sound of the train's brakes grabbed the tracks and the loud horn began blaring. The ground shook something fierce below my feet, and the horn blared, piercing my ears. My heart pounded so hard it hurt my chest, but I smiled nonetheless.

I was about to yell out "Hello!" to her, when a clasp of bony fingers clutched my upper arm and yanked me off the tracks. His clumsy jerk of my body forced us into a rapid rocky run down the gravel mound. He continued to pull me by the arm and away from the tracks as I tried desperately to break loose from his grasp, but I was overpowered. He managed to pull me alongside him.

"Didn't you hear me, young lady?" the old man yelled into my ear, competing with the thunderous roar of the train.

The Portland Rose roared from behind and pulled the air around us. I stopped and his clutch loosened. I closed my eyes tightly and imagined that her engine arms had reached out, grabbed me from the old man's tight grasp, and thrown me underneath her wings. I waited and waited as I felt the breath of each boxcar pass by me. Eventually, the air went silent.

I slowly opened my watering eyes and found the old man looking directly at me. At first, his eyes revealed a dark ugly glare, then widened in dismay upon seeing my face and he dropped his grasp.

"Well," he said, wiping the dress as if there was dirt on it, "at least you're alright."

I said nothing.

"What's…um, your name?" His voice was hoarse.

My head dropped. "Michael Richardson…Junior, sir."

"Ah, I see," he said. "You're Judge Richardson's boy."

He lifted my chin and gave a half smile,

"Well, son, do you have other clothes underneath there?" He tugged at the dress.

I nodded.

"Well then, it would probably be best to get you home in those underneath clothes. Don't you think?"

I walked over to where I had left my Buster Brown

shoes and kicked off the pink heels, unzipped the back of the dress and pulled it over my head.

"Probably best we just leave those here, son," he said kindly.

I dropped my mother's dress and pink heels on the ground and walked slowly back to the old man without looking at him.

"Alright, let's get you home." His voice had sounded like he had caught me doing some foolish boy antic. He had no idea it was no happenstance incident or, maybe, he really didn't want to know.

The old man wrapped his feeble arm around my shoulders in fatherly fashion and gently guided me all the way home. When we had arrived, he told my mother to keep a better eye on me, but he did not tell her what had occurred.

"Remember what I told you," he said, winking at me and then tipping his hat as he walked away. But, to this day, I do not remember what he told me.

We had walked for what had seemed like forever and, though the old man talked on, I had not listened to his words. I was too focused on my thoughts of how one day I was going to go back to those tracks. However, I had convinced myself that the next time would be the last time—no matter what it took.

I had always known I was not like others. Although I had been born with all the appropriate boy appendages, I knew deep down I was truly meant to be a girl. Maybe there was some mix up in the souls of heaven's exit gate, or maybe like someone born with six toes, it just happens. Whatever the reason, it had never mattered much to me that I was a girl on the inside. But to my father, the Honorable Judge Richardson, I was to be an all-American boy a hundred percent of the time, even if he had to beat it into me.

I had tried hard to fit in with boys in the neighborhood and at school, but I never did. They wanted to fight and wrestle and were always up to juvenile mischief. They found spitting and punching funny. I found it atrocious. Besides, I already had plenty for the boys to tease me about with a pair of oversized ears that stuck out like television antennas and a nose twice the size of my face. I was a scrawny and clumsy kid – never the first pick in any sport. On the playground, I would always watch the girls and wanted so much to be with them. My looming at them actually helped me in a way, because the boys mistakenly thought I was "girl" crazy.

I had learned at a young age that any urges to be a girl needed concealed. My father would rather I lay dead than to even mention any talk of my girl tendencies. When I was six years old, my mother had taken me to our neighbor's house. The women had all sat in the kitchen talking away while I played dolls with Abby and Maggie. Their brothers were playing baseball outside. For some reason, my father had gotten home early that day and had come over to let mother know. He had not seen me playing with the boys and immediately asked her where I was. I could hear the fear in mother's voice as she pretended like she didn't know. I heard him coming down the hallway and then he barged into Abby's room to find me having a tea party with the two girls and the dolls. He stormed over, grabbed me by the back of the collar, and dragged me outside to their front porch,

"You never, and I mean NEVER, play with dolls. Do you understand me boy?" I tried not to cry because he would have hit me if I did.

"Now go play with the boys." He shoved me roughly off the porch and I ran over to where they were playing. The boys were at least nice enough to include me until my father was out of sight then they told me to go away. They knew, as much as I did, that I was different.

I had tried to be a boy as much as possible to please my father, but the older I got the harder it was to continue the charade. So I gave in, knowing I had to do it secretly. I had found a flowered yellow sheet and yellow pillowcase in the guest bedroom closet. I cut up the seam on one side of the pillowcase and used it to put on my head like long hair – beautiful blonde hair.

My mother used to bring home *Good Housekeeping* magazines with illustrated covers of smiling woman dressed beautifully on them. I would pour over the pages when no one was around. The magazines had articles on hair and fashion, and house cleaning ads with women wearing pretty dresses and heels. They all seemed so happy. When mother threw out the magazines, I would dig them out of the trash, wrap them in my yellow sheet, and hide them under my bed.

At night, when my parents thought I was asleep, I would get up and put on my hair, wrap myself in the sheet, imagining it was a dress, and then twirl around. I would pretend to be one of the ladies in the magazines and that the other ladies were my friends who called me Michelle. I was able to hide this fantasy for a while. Then one day, while I was at school, my mother found my girl stockpile.

I don't know why she told my father, but she did and he stormed into my room. I jumped to my feet. He was waving one of the magazines in the air.

"Why are these under your bed?" he yelled, "Why?"

I looked at my feet, and mumbled to myself.

"What did you say?" he demanded angrily and my head shot up.

"I said I like the way the women dress," I repeated defiantly.

"What do you mean you like the way they dress?" his voice lowered. "Because you think they're pretty?" he continued. "Right? Yes, that's it. Now that's my boy! Now all we need to do is get you playing ball."

"No, Father." I shook my head. "I don't want to play ball."

"Don't be a fool. All boys want to play ball, some just aren't as good as the others, that's all."

"No!" I yelled. "I do not want to play ball."

"Yes, you do, now stop being stupid."

"I'm not stupid, I don't want to play ball, and I don't look at the magazine because I like girls, Father. I look at them because I want to be a girl."

The back of his hand flew across my face like a bat to a baseball and I sailed across the room, hitting the dresser first, then the floor. He stormed over to me and his fingers wrapped around my throat as he picked me up by the neck and thrust me up against the wall.

"You listen to me real good, boy. Never!" His grasp shook my body. "I mean, never will you speak like that again!"

His fingers tightened as I struggled for air.

 "Or I swear to Christ that I will beat you so damn hard that your own mother wouldn't even recognize you. Do you understand me?"

I continued to gasp for air as tears streamed heavily down my face. And with that he let go and my ten-year-old body fell to the floor. The old man found me standing on those railroad tracks the next day.

I curled up in a cocoon after that. I ate very little and lost a lot of weight. I was put in the hospital twice for dehydration. My mother worried incessantly about my weight and began to secretly cut out and give me pictures from her magazines, as long as I agreed to eat them after looking at them. It helped a little, but my marks in school were so bad, that by the end of that school year, I wound up being held back a year. That's when I met Johnny Lewis.

He was a known troublemaker, and a loner, too. Johnny's mother died at his birth, which sent his father into an alcoholic downward spiral and why he was well known as the town drunk. He was also the mayor, so everyone looked the other way, especially when Johnny was causing problems. I don't remember how Johnny and I had become friends, but by Thanksgiving, we were hanging out all the time. I remember this mostly because it was on Thanksgiving Day that Johnny and I began the first of our many house break-ins.

Johnny and I had been walking down the street in silence, for neither of us wanted to talk about our turkey day. The Baxters had walked out of their house with their perfect little daughter and son in tow, happy and holding hands. It was like a Norman Rockwell painting and something about it set my soul on fire – and Johnny's, too.

"I wish I could bash those smiles off their faces," I blurted as we watched the Baxters drive off.

Johnny looked at me shocked, then laughed. "If I could and get away with it, I would."

"I bet they wouldn't be so smiley if they came back and their perfect little home wasn't so perfect."

Johnny stopped. 'What are you talking about?"

"Come on," I smirked. "I will show you what I'm talking about."

I darted toward the Baxter's house and Johnny followed. We went through their back yard and, luckily, they had left the back door unlocked. As we walked in, I immediately saw a baseball bat on the floor and picked it up. Johnny found a golf club in the closet. We destroyed everything in sight.

On our way out, I grabbed one of Mrs. Baxter's dresses. I made fun of it so Johnny wouldn't think it weird.

"You taking that with you?" he asked.

I played it off. "Sure, why not? I need a souvenir. Something to remind me of what I think her face will look like when she's walks back into the perfect little home she keeps so tidy."

Johnny laughed. "I want a souvenir, too." And he went straight to the liquor cabinet.

The next day it was all over town about the "poor Baxters." Johnny and I laughed as we read the newspaper in my tree house.

"What did you do with that dress anyway?" he asked.

"It's in that chest." I pointed at the brown box tucked in the corner. "Under lock and key."

He nodded. "Good idea. So who's next?"

"Next?" I asked.

"We can't stop now. We have the whole town wound up!"

Johnny was right. We did have the town in fear, *and* with only one house break-in. Something about it felt real good.

"We need to be smart about it, Johnny. We need a plan."

That day we wrote up our strategy—the who's, when's, and where's. For almost a year, we ran havoc on the town. We only hit one house a month, although a couple of times we waited for two months because we were afraid of getting caught. No one had suspected us, and because Johnny had stopped getting into trouble, everyone chalked it up to me being a good influence on him. The town was convinced it was someone else, such as a man from out of town, but only because they were sure no one capable of such violence lived among them.

I had quite the collection of dresses. I had several wigs now and some lipsticks, too, although Johnny didn't know about that. Whenever possible, I would go to my tree house and dress up.

It was a blistering hot summer day and Johnny and I had been down at the lake earlier. Johnny hadn't been feeling too well from being hung over, so we had headed home early. I had been fine with leaving early anyway because I wanted to get to my tree house to have time to myself. However, went I got home, I could hear someone mulling around in my tree house. At first, I thought it was one of the neighbor kids, but then I heard the enraged cursing of my father. I knew immediately he had broken into my chest.

I was furious and headed his way. I was going to kill him. I was going to take the bat and beat him in the head. All I wanted was to see blood coming from his skull.

He had been throwing items everywhere and yelling so loud that he didn't hear me come in. I grabbed the baseball bat leaning next to the door and before I had a chance to give it a second thought, I swung the bat at his head. But my father turned around in that moment and caught the bat with his hand.

"I hate you!" I yelled. "I wish you were dead!"

He paused for a moment then said, "That makes two of us."

He pushed me out of the way and climbed down out of the tree house. I stayed in there until it got too cold, then made my way to my bedroom. The next morning when I returned to the tree house, everything was gone.

"Come on, Michael," my father said from behind me. "Let's go."

I wasn't aware we were planning on going anywhere but I did what he instructed and got in the car. We drove for miles and said nothing to each other. I finally fell asleep. I awoke to my car door opening and a man dressed in white pulling me out. I tried to speak, but nothing came out. I was frozen with fear. I knew where I was and knew what was about to happen. I did not attempt to look for my father. I allowed the two orderlies to walk me in and I never saw my father again.

I had been there for two years when my mother came to visit me for the first time. She looked old and tired and much thinner with gray streaking through her hair. She didn't say much, except that she found the institution disgusting and no place for anyone to be in.

"How's Johnny?" I asked.

She hesitated for a moment. "Johnny's dead, Michael."

"What? What happened?"

"He was out of control after you left. You were real good for him, you know. Everyone said that. But soon after you were gone, he lost it. It was very sad. Then one day, no one knew why really, he stole a car and parked it on the railroad tracks and the train took him. Very sad."

The Portland Rose had gotten Johnny.

My mother did not stay for long and it was the last time I ever saw her. Although, I am sure my mother had something to do with the fact I was sent here to Emerson a month later.

It was great here at first. Dr. Huxley was amazing and accepted me for who and what I am. He let me wear dresses and make up and, here, I was normal. Dr. Huxley and I had accepted that I would never have a chance outside of these walls, so I become a part of the inside where I was safe. However, that all changed after he died and Dr. V took over.

Now, every week is survival for me. For I know that I am

one of Dr. V's "special" projects. They are giving me something. I don't know what it is, but my body is turning muscular and hair is growing on my face and chest where it had never been before. They are giving me something that makes my appearance more masculine. I suppose they believe they can make me a "man." I know there is a reason he lets me continue to wear my dresses and make up. He has me talking to that Dr. Franks every week. They are collecting data, so that is what I give them. Most of it I make up as I go along and then leave out something at the end of each session.

"I just can't talk about it anymore, doctor." I throw out my fake tears. "It's real hard for me to talk about this right now." I cross my legs and place my hands on my knees. "But next week, next week I will tell you more."

He comes over to the couch, puts his arm around me and slides his hand up my skirt. "Maybe the doctor can make things better?" he whispers then kisses my face.

"Not yet," I screech like a girl. "I'm not ready yet."

Then I pat down my skirt. I will never be ready for that, but every week I have to play the game. I have to have them wanting to know more because when the notes are done, I will be, too. I know they want to take out my brain and see what makes a man think that he is woman. I am sure Dr. Franks will want to have his sexual ways with me before that as well, which makes my stomach hurl and my head ache.

Every day is worse. They do not let me shave my legs and arms like Dr. Huxley allowed. I look hideous with hairy arms and legs protruding from my dress. Every morning, a nurse comes in and asks if I want to wear a shirt with pants or a dress. And although my hairy body is repulsing, I put on the dress. I know if I wear the "man" clothes, then they have won – and I will be done for.

This has become a chess match with death. Each move I

make is crucial. I must make them think they are dominating the board. I play the pawn. However, the game cannot last forever; the pieces are slowly coming off the board. So when I heard of Sabel's plan, I went to Jackie. I told her I must leave and will do whatever it takes to get out of here. Ironic, I suppose, that I tried so hard to kill myself all those times and now I am doing everything I can to stay alive.

So, I am in with them, Dr. Quill. I have nothing to lose at this point. I fantasize about how, on the night of the revolution, I will track down that quack and look him in the eyes with an army of patients behind me and declare, "Checkmate."

I know we are on an island and that the existence of Emerson Rose is unknown to others. I suppose Dr. V and his crew think our hidden existence keeps them safe from others finding out about what they do to the patients in here. What's funny is that they have never thought about the fact that it can also keep us loonies safe from anyone ever knowing what we do to them.

With great sincerity,

Michael Richards, Jr.

4

PRAY TELL

Dear Dr. Quill,

My name is Juliette and I have been a patient here at the Emerson Rose Asylum for nearly ten years now, though I hope to be leaving soon, *(if all goes as planned)* for this place is not where I belong. A long time ago, there was a priest, a gun, and a vengeance that placed me here.

You see, a blue plaid skirt is easy access to a white collared man in black. He had already been teaching my older brother since the age of ten. You learn many lessons in a school like that. Like, a child is only to be seen, not heard.

"Do not say a word about this," I was told.

Shh…in the name of the father… his son…and the

Holy Spirit.

I said nothing. Who would have listened? After papa died, mother threw herself like a sacrificial lamb into the church of Catholic heathens. She spent more time with those church laden hypocrites than with my brother and me. The worst part was the way my mother and those churchies followed Father Tom around as if he was the Pied Piper. He ruled all of them and not a one of them would have so much as crapped in the toilet without first asking Father Tom when, where, or how.

Yes, Mrs. Johnson, you may go rid yourself of bodily fluids…now go n' pee.

…and I can tell you that none of them wanted to know what Father Tom was really doing with his flute.

I was lucky, in a way, because even though I was only eight years old, I could block it all out. My brother, however, could not seem to block any of it out. I learned quickly to recite the Serenity Prayer in my head as I thought of things like playing with my Crissy doll or having a huge ice cream sundae all to myself. I never let myself really be there, but my brother could not seem to escape in any way. I guess years of that would get to any boy.

When my brother turned thirteen, things began to get bad. Purposely, he would get into trouble for stealing, fighting, and cutting class in an attempt to get himself kicked out of school. Instead, the principal, Sister Teresa, became fed up and made my brother go on a weekend retreat with Father Tom. The very night my brother returned home, he went straight to his bedroom and shot himself in the head.

I remember that night. I heard the gun go off, though it had sounded more like a soda can popped. Then I heard my mother scream and I knew. I ran to his room and saw mother leaned over his body, rocking and praying. Her screaming cries pierced my ears. I stood in the doorway staring at his head. There was a hole and blood poured like lava. His brown eyes were bulging and staring back at me. I wanted to say something to him but mother turned around and screamed for me to call the ambulance. At the time, I had thought was stupid because he was already dead. What was taking him to the hospital going to do?

The police arrived shortly thereafter and my mother went to the front door. I ran to his room quickly, looking for his note, but I found nothing. When I heard them coming towards the bedroom, I darted back to mine at the end of the hall. I heard my mother sobbing while the officer tried asking questions. Officer Brown came into my room where I had been on the floor with my Crissy doll. I had just pulled the rubber band from her long ponytail and was giving her a haircut.

"Funny thing," Officer Brown said and sat on the floor across from me. "We can't seem to find the gun. Do you know anything about that?"

I tried to think of why he thought that was a funny thing and kept playing with my doll. "No sir. I don't know where the gun is. Did you look real good?"

"Yes, yes we did."

"Did you find a note from my brother?" I demanded to know.

"No, no note." He sighed. "I know this is all confusing, but they don't always leave a note..."

I threw down my doll, pointed the scissors at him and shouted, "He was supposed to leave a note! Don't you understand? He was supposed to leave a note!"

"I'm sorry, honey." Officer Brown gently grabbed my hand with the scissors and I let go, "This is one of those things that, in spite of all my years, I will never understand."

Of course, he did not understand. Why would he? My brother swore he would explain everything, but he didn't. He left me there to take it all. Why didn't he leave a note? My brother had told me that he would kill himself one day. He wanted to die because of what was being done to him and he was to leave a note explaining that it was also being done to me. I wanted it to stop so bad that I did not stop my brother. His suicide was to be my salvation.

His death was more painful than I thought it would be. I should have said something, I should have done something, but I didn't. I hate myself for that.

Right after his funeral, I began to act real bad myself. I would have erratic outbreaks and spontaneously throw things or punch other kids for no reason. Sister Teresa said if I did not behave, she would send me on a weeklong retreat with Father Tom to have the devil *taken out of me*. However, the way I saw it, Father Tom was the devil and he needed to be *taken out of me*. That was how I ended up here.

Things here at Emerson Rose were really good at first, when Dr. Huxley was still alive. He even gave me a new Crissy doll one Christmas, but in time, I wasn't allowed to cut her hair unless someone was around. That's because one time I was in the recreation room on the floor with my Crissy doll and the hair mechanism stuck. No matter how hard I yanked, the hair would not pull out. I became so angry I threw the doll down then took the scissors and started to slash my arms. One of the nurses ran over and grabbed the scissors from me and yelled for another nurse to come and help. Dr. Huxley had walked in at that moment.

I looked up at him and began to cry. "Take the devil out of me," I begged him as the nurse began to wrap a bandage around my slashed arm.

Dr. Huxley squatted and looked me in the eyes. "There is no devil in you," he said in a matter of fact tone, "Juliette, evil is on the outside and will only infect the inside if you let it."

After that, I did good with not letting evil thoughts get to me. Dr. Huxley had me take medication that helped and I could talk to him every Wednesday at 8:00 a.m., if I needed. Then, Dr. Huxley introduced me to theater because he said I had a flare for the dramatics, which meant he thought I would be good in acting. I was always the star in our Romeo and *Juliette* because Dr. Huxley joked I was born to play the part. Dr. Huxley would direct and we were allowed to perform for the other patients. That was always a big night here; even the patients would dress up in nice clothes to see our performances. Those were the happiest moments in my life…ever. Then, then he was gone and it all changed.

They say Dr. Huxley died of a heart attack. I'm not so sure because he had the best heart ever. Anyway, he was gone and all of a sudden, Dr. Vanodin was here and that's when things got bad for me. I haven't told anyone about it, though. I don't talk about the demons that come to my room at night. I've seen what this place does to others who tell about the things they see. The orderlies come and take them away in the middle of the night. Sometimes I think they take their brain, because their minds are gone by morning. I hear them at night, dragging others out of their rooms. I don't want to be hauled off and taken to the other side of the wall, but these two demons that come at night… well, they are getting really bad and I want them gone.

I don't know the names of these two demons, or if they even have names, but I call them Spike and Scorch. The demons only stand about one to two feet tall and perch on my metal footboard like vultures. For the most part, they look alike with dark red lizard-like skin and clawed feet that clamp to my bed foot rail. They have skinny calves with bulky thighs and their lower backs curve in up to shoulders that hunch over. They have muscular biceps, tiny forearms and their hands look much like their feet, with pointy black nails. Their oversized mouths are packed with long jagged teeth and their yellow glowing eyes have pupils like black marbles.

Spike, however, has mirrored silver stubby spikes all over his back and on the top of his head. He doesn't say much, really, but it's a mild ear piercing hissing noise when he does. Spike mostly just laughs like some kind of obnoxious hyena and it is annoying, more than anything else is.

Then there's Scorch. I hate that demon and want to rip

his head off. He has a big wrinkled head with two crusty brown horns protruding from the forehead. The rest of his head is covered with what looks like petrified red, orange and black fire flames. He squints at me all the time and his mouth never shuts up. Scorch talks a lot about stuff I don't understand but I am sure it's mean. I try to ignore him but when I do, he just gets louder and meaner. At first, I was able to ignore them, but lately it's becoming more and more unbearable. Like last night, when Scorch started in on me. "Juliette…Juliette! Juuulieeette. Wake up! Wake up! Wake up, Juliette. Wake up! Wake up! Wake, wake, wake up, Juliette. Wake up!"

"What?" I popped up.

"The snake misses his home, you know. For the man loves a lamb much his youth to endure his old age."

"You're stupid," I yelled and lay back down.

I heard Spike say, "Juliette, Juliette!"

Scorch snickered. "A jar needs its pickle from the garden so ripe for my dearest, I fearest you are a female friendless, useless."

"Sss, picklesss, picklesss, hsss!" Spike snorted a laugh as he clapped his hands.

I shook my head, grasped my blanket, and closed my eyes.

"Wake up! Wake up! Wake up, Juliette," Scorch yelled as he and Spike start clacking on the bedrail with their foot claws louder and louder,

Spike's laugh screeched and it began to burn my ears. I put the pillow over my head tight, but it didn't help,

I popped up and screamed, "Shut up! Will you two just shut up! God, you're both so stupid!"

They cackled and suddenly my door began to open. I threw myself under the covers quickly.

"What's going on in here?" the night guard demanded. I pretended to be asleep.

I heard the guard slap his baton. "If I hear one more peep out of you, I will be back," he threatened then stepped out and shut the door.

Spike and Scorch came back, laughing. "Hey, Juliette the big brawny guard man wants to use his stick on you."

"Ssstick, hsss, hsss..."

"I do not know why he would want to use his stick on you," Scorch scoffed. "You look like some pathetic pauper boy with that chopped off haircut of yours, but maybe he likes boys, Juliette. Do you think he likes boys?"

"Boysss, he likesss, boysss!" Spike snickered.

"Well, then, isn't that guard going to have quite the surprise when he finds this boy has boobies!"

Spike burst into laughter so hard his body shook the bed. He also tried to say something, but instead began to choke. I smiled just for a second. However, I did not want the guard to come back so I let the demons have their words. Scorch ranted on and Spike laughed as I just laid there with thoughts of my Crissy doll and ice cream sundaes. I did not dare fight back. I did that one time and, believe me, I will never do that again. It happened the other night. I had been in a deep sleep when Scorch woke me up and started ranting.

"Deceitful the face! Deceitful the heart! And man is man, we doest forget..." Scorch was talking in a high-pitched tone that pierced my ears and Spike's laugh was louder, more irritating than ever. I was so exhausted and could not take it anymore. I came out from under my covers very angry, crawled right up to the foot rail, and looked Scorch in the eyes.

I pointed my finger right in his face and sternly declared, "Listen hear, you little prick, I am sick and tired of your bullshit and I am not going to take it anymore." Then I brusquely backhanded Scorch right in the mouth. He flipped backwards off the rail and fell hard onto the floor. Spike laughed so hysterically that I began to laugh, too. Scorch scurried right back up the foot rail within seconds and snarled. Scorch stood completely upright, which stretched him a foot taller. He firmly crossed his arms and looked down at me with wide eyes.

"Oh my, little Juliette, don't be so upset my dear," Scorch said, but it was not his voice; it was Fathers Tom's voice and I froze. "You are an angel sent to me, that is why we must be one, my little Juliette. Shh...."

My body shook uncontrollably and my eyes spilled tears.

"Oh my, sweet girl, do not be afraid..."

I quickly jumped out of bed, grabbed the pillow, and yanked the blanket off. I darted to the corner of the room and threw the blanket over my entire body. I curled up into a fetal position with my pillow, sobbing until I fell asleep. The next morning, I awoke in my bed with my pillow and blanket. I never confronted Scorch again.

I miss Dr. Huxley so much. He was such a nice man and never asked me about the past. The demons were not here then. They did not show up until Dr. Vanodin arrived and made me start talking to that stupid crusty old psychiatrist who looks like he has one foot in the grave. All they want is to know everyone's secrets here, but I only talk about my brother's death. I know I have to say something to them, because if I give them nothing, they will do what they can do to pull something out of me.

I wish I could talk to someone about the demons, but I cannot. I have become so delirious with lack of sleep and I feel like my soul is draining out of me. I can't tell them about the demons, but I can't take it anymore either, so when Sabel asked for help to escape, I quickly said yes. She has already rounded up many of the other patients to be part of the plan. The great part is that I am an important part since Dr. V lets me work in his office. I go every Friday and spend the day filing. I do not say anything, I just file and Dr. V ignores me. It's not that he's nice to me, but he's not mean to me either. He even told me one day that I did a good job. I thanked him then asked what made him chose me for the job. Dr. V said it was because I knew how to keep a secret and he was right, I do. For I had never told anyone, not even Dr. Huxley, what Father Tom did to me or about the day I went and avenged my brother's death.

It was on a Saturday evening, ten years ago, and Father Tom was preparing for the next day's sermon at the church's altar. I walked in through the front double doors and he quickly turned to face me, the altar now behind him. I had worn my uniform special for that day and skipped happily down the aisle. I could feel my brown curls bounce on my white collared blouse. I smiled with my hands behind my back and Father Tom smiled in return. When I got to the edge of the maroon carpet steps, I stopped, batted my big brown eyes, then pulled the gun from behind my back and shot him right in the penis.

He doubled over and dropped to his knees with one hand holding his groin and his other hand stretched towards me for help. His watery eyes begged for mercy as he tried to say my name but he choked instead. I threw the gun on the floor, turned around and walked back down the aisle, smiling as I repeatedly recited louder and louder, "God grant me the serenity to accept the things I cannot change, courage to change the things I can; and wisdom to know the difference…"

When I reached the double doors, I heard a flurry of people surrounding Father Tom as they yelled for towels and a doctor. I strutted out, down the cement steps, and skipped happily down the street until I reached the park on the other side of town, where I found a bench and slept on it for the night.

The next morning, I was awakened by a police officer shaking me. "Wake up, wake up, Juliette." I groggily sat up and the officer put his coat around me. "C'mon, kid, it's time to go."

I realized at that moment that it was Officer Brown. There was a moment of hesitation when I looked up into his eyes and, for just a split second, I thought he was going to tell me to make a run for it. Instead, he put me into the back seat of his patrol car and took me straight to the local hospital. Within a couple of days, I was shipped here to Emerson.

At the time, I thought I would be out of this asylum soon. I thought the churchies would understand what happened and that my mother would come and get me out. I thought the note I had left explaining what Father Tom had done to my brother would bestow my redemption, but I never received my emancipation. Maybe I should have told them in the note that he did that to me, too, and then maybe they would have understood.

It doesn't matter now, though, because I will be out of this place soon enough. I cannot wait until the night when Spike and Scorch show up on my bed rail and find that I am not there. I would love to see the looks on their astonished faces. In fact, until I leave this place, I will no longer think of my doll or an ice cream sundae when they start to badger me.

Instead, I will now imagine the night when Spike and Scorch find me gone. I will envision that I have stuffed my pillow under the covers so they will think I am there. And Scorch will start in.

"Wake up, Juliette, wake up!"

Yet there will be no answer.

Scorch will go on one of his tangents and when not even a breath comes out of me, Scorch and Spike will become so enraged that they will jump onto the bed and scamper to the headboard. Scorch will yank the covers down, and they will discover I am gone. Spike will go silent and Scorch's head of flames will ignite like a bonfire.

I will picture myself sitting on the foot rail, visible to their eyes. They will hear shrills of laughter, which will make them freeze. Then their bodies will turn into paper and fall flat onto the bed. I will then jump to the floor and walk around to the side of the bed.

"Well, well, well," I will pronounce as I pick them up. "Let us play a game of rock, paper…" And I will pull out my scissors, cutting them into a hundred pieces all over the bed. Once done, I scoop them up and throw them in the air and, like a confetti shower; they will fall on me as I turn in circles verbosely rejoicing, "God grant me the serenity to accept the things I cannot change; courage to change the things I can; and wisdom to know the difference."

After that, I will lie down on the bed and fall asleep and awaken on that park bench with Officer Brown shaking me.

"Wake up, wake up, Juliette," Officer Brown will say as I sit up groggily while he puts the coat around me.

"C'mon, kid, it's time to go," he will say.

Then I look into his eyes and stand up, and Officer Brown will declare, "Run, kid. Run and never come back."

And I will do just that.

A glooming peace will then overtake me, the sun will show their evil heads no more, go will I, to have no more talk of these sad things, for never shall there be told the woes of me, Juliette.

With Warmest Regards,

Juliette

5

MOE BETTER

Dear Sir,

My name is Moe. Wells, my reals name's Morris but my ma called mes Moe. Some call mes "Crazy Moe" but I ain't crazy, sir. They says I am crazy cuz sometimes I gets real mad and that's makes me hurt someone. I don't hurt no one, sir, though, unless they'd gone and did something real mean. I tell them, "You best stop now, before I gets real mad."

They think cuz I don't talk real good, cuz I stutter, that I'm stupid, but I ain't stupid, sir. Cuz I smarts enough to know how to knocks them out. Don't knows why theys be mean like that and I gets in trouble for it. Don't seem fair to me. Maybe cuz I colored or cuz I'm bigger, stronger than thems, but I old too and theys know that. I thinks they get to be mean cuz they works here, but I'm gettin tired of that, sir.

One time, one of them orderlies, I hurt him bad, but I just couldn't stop, sir. I just couldn't. My hands just felt good on his neck. His face turned red and blew up like a balloon. Kinda made me laugh. Then I felt a big thump on my head and I fell off him. Nurse Dunsberrys had whacked me with a baseball bat. I rolled onto my back and looked up. Nurse Dunberrys held that bat high over me, waitin' to swing likes I was some kind of rodent runnings lose in her kitchen. I just gets real mad sometimes when things are said and whens I can't take it no more. If they wouldn't say mean things, I wouldn't gets so mad.

My dad would gets mad like that, but he'd been drinking whiskey. His friends would play cards and drink all night on the front porch. When they'd get real drunks, pa would call me out from bed. Is only nine then. He'd tell me to say words he knew I couldn't say cuz I'd stutter real bad. Then him and his friends would laugh real hard and throw rocks at me sayings I was retarded. The mores I couldn't say things, the harder they'd throw them rocks at me.

They'd say things like, "Hey, retard, say Peter Piper picked a peck of pickled peppers."

I'd try real hard, but words with a lot p's is real hard for me and their laughing would makes me mess it up. I learned not to cry though, no, sir. I'm real good at not crying. I would get knocked to the moon if I had any tears. No crying, I held it in real good, Dr. Quill.

I wasn't always this way. I was real smart when I real little. Ma said when I was seven years old and hits by a car it musta messed up my brain some. She said I just wasn't the same after that, but she said she loved me all the same. Made no difference to her. I asked her one time if pa loved me, too, after my brain gots messed up. Ma smiled and tolds me, "Don't you mind that pa of yours, he's just a cranky ole man. Don't you pay him any attention, son."

She hugged me tight and told me to go play with my friends, but she knew I hadn't no friends.

I had two older sisters and one older brother, but theys didn't like me either. They'd tell me the retard stork broughts me by mistake. That I supposed to go to retard town. They weres embarrassed of me and pretend theys didn't know me when others were around. They'd be mean to me in front of pa cuz he thoughts it was real funny. Though Ma slapped them all in the back of the heads if she'd catched 'em doing that's to me.

Then Ma died and things changed real bad. Pa drunk more and more. I gots hit more and mores. Pa yelled at me, sayin he didn't need one more mouth to feed. So I promised I wouldn't eat and I didn't even eats a crumb. That only lasted a few days though and one night pa drug me out of bed, tied my hands behinds my back and then puts a potato sack overs my head. He tied it on real tight and puts me in the car. We drove for a long, long time. He yelled at me the whole way and was sayings I was retarded and other words, sir, I wills not write. He said I'd killed my mother cuz I was so retarded she couldn't stand it no mores. Then he stopped, shoved me outs the car, and yelled, "Don't you ever come back! None of us wants you! No one wants a retard!"

I heard the door slam shut and his car drive off real fast. The next morning some nice man found me and tooks me to the police. The police were real nice to me but they said they had to puts me ins an orphanage.

I was good for a couple years at that orphanage. There was a real nice lady there. Her name was Miss Dolly. She liked me and told me I smart. She showed me how to read and writes.

Miss Dolly gots me to the third level and said that was real good. She had pretty blonde hair in a bun and smiled like an angel. Whenever I'd gets real mad at myself she'd always tell me, "Now, Morris, take a deep breath and count to ten real slow."

Miss Dolly told me it was real important for me to not get so mads. She said I was reals big and had a deep louds voice for a twelve years old. I looked likes a twenty year old she said and my strength could make me real harmful if I let my anger gets the best of me. She said that I didn't knows my own strength and I had to be real careful cuz it was a gift for good things not bad. I 've tried to think of that a lot so I don't get so mad but I just can't help it sometimes, sir, my thoughts go away and I just lose my minds.

Then Miss Dolly had to move. Her husband had found a real good job somewheres far and Miss Dolly couldn't teach me no more. She had tears on her last day and that made me have some tears, too. I said sorry for having tears and she hugged me and said it was okay for me to have tears. I cried so hard I couldn't make them tears stop and my body shook likes there was a big earthquake. Miss Dolly sat me down and rocked me until my tears went dry. Then rights before she left, she told me to remembers I was real special.

After that, the kids at the orphanage started to tease me reals bad. I had worked so hard, sir, getting my stuttering gone but their teasing made me so mad it camed back. So did my anger. One day, I was sittin by myself reading outside when a boy named Billy and his friends camed over. They'd started calling me names and I paid them no never mind at first. Then Billy picked up some rocks and began throwing at me harder and harder. The other boys began to laughs and that made me so mad.

I jump up, charged at Billy and threw hims to the gravel. My knees pinned him down and I forced his mouth open by puttin' my hand around his jaw. Then with my other hand, I shoved gravel and rocks down his mouth. I was putting them in there real good.

Billy choked hard and tried to squirm away but I held hims down real good. Guess one of the boys ran off to tell cuz Mr. Connors and the janitor came from behind and yanked me off Billy. I laughed so hard as they rolled Billy onto his stomach and he spit out all those rocks. Mr. Connors and the janitor took me to a room and locked me up. I was there 'til someone picked me up and then I sent here.

Don't know if you knows, Dr. Quill, but I been here longer than you. Dr. Huxley said I the first of his special projects. I wasn't from rich families like the others that were heres then. Most of them gots to go home and Dr. Huxley said he was getting those who's didn't have no homes to go back to. I got here right before you but I didn't get to come out til Dr. Huxley knew I'd be real good. He told me I was the goodest man he'd ever did know and if that angry side got out of me, he said I would be a real good part of this place. And he did, Dr. Quill, he helped me real good. No one teased me here then. Dr Huxley would have none of that, no sir. The nurses and others that were here then was real nice. Then that Dr. V showed up and my angry part cames back and it's cames back real bad.

It started whens Dr. V had me diggin' holes for trees theys planting around the new parts of the building. I just started diggin' a hole when this orderly came out for a smokes break and started makin' funs of me.

'Hey, stu-stu-stupid," he yelled and come ups behind me.

I told hims to stop before I gots mad, but he just kepta talkin.

"Ah, you want me to shu-shu-shut up you stupid negro?"

That made me so mads that I swung around with the shovel and knocked that skinny lil white boy in the head reals hard. He fell like a sack a potatoes and laid there notta movin. I turned around and kepta digging. When I done, I'd went inside and told a nurse he's out there. I don't knows what happened to him. I didn't see him after that but they came for me that night and drug me out my room. They hooked me ups to some machine with wires and saids theys gonna shock me.

I was real scared at first and tried to get out of the chair but they had my hands strapped downs real good. Then they turned the machine on and it made a funny noise but it didn't hurts me at first. The nurses and Chinese doctor started getting real noisy, talkin' almost likes theys excited and I just kept sitting there. One of the nurses kepta saying more, more, and thens they'd talk an' and writes stuff down. Theys been doin' it to me every night now and its startin to hurts real bad cuz they keeps puttin me in that chair longer and longer each times and I don't likes it one bit, no sir.

Theys still let me do the yard work 'round here, but one times they's had me helpin' them cookers. Them cooking folks are meaner than them orderlies. Cuz I helpin 'em by puttin' boxes in their big freezer and when I puts the last box in, theys locked me in the freezer. Theys thinking theys funny doing that and then I don't know how it happened but theys forgot I in there.

I guess I lucky the night guard checked my room that night. They had a mad search thinkin I'd gone and escaped. Then Dr. V's dog had sniffed me out. The orderlies pulled me out the freezer then threw me in my room. Dr. V had a couple of 'em night guards beat me with their sticks to show me a lesson. I was too frozen to fights back anyway. I still don't feel my toes real good.

What they do to us here, sir, just aint right. I know I ain't perfect the way I gets mad but I don't sets out to be mean just to be mean. Theys do though. So whens Jackie camed and asked me to help her and that black haired girl, I said yes. I figure the ways Dr. V keeps frying me likes a chicken, they ain't gonna stop til they kills me. I aint stupid, sir.

I been collecting rocks every times they have me do the yard work. I puts a little in my pockets then when I gets to my room, I put them in a hole I tore in my mattress. Almost gots enough to shove in all of their mouths and shut them up reals good. Theys gonna be real surprised, Dr. Quill, when we gets them. We gonna show them. They may thinks we aint so right in the head, but we gonna shows them that we aint so wrongs in the head either.

God bless you, sir,

Moe

6

THE MUTE IN ME

March 25, 1978

Dear Dr. Quill,

    I look outside my bedroom window and see the plush grass. So green and vibrant, yet peaceful. The trees are strong and sturdy, yet topped with such delicate frail leaves. Do you enjoy such scenery, Doctor? Funny how no one ever declares a tree or grass, or even a storm of clouds crazy. When the elements act out of their realm of normal, no one calls them insane; they simply call it nature. That is what we are here, to me, the purest form of nature – the cyclone, the tsunami, the hurricane. A beautiful disaster.

    I am writing to you for there is a lot of respect for the words that you speak around here. I myself speak with no words. They call me a mute. Although, a mute is one unable to speak and I suppose I have the ability to speak, but I have not tried and I have no desire to do so.

    They treat me as if I am incompetent. I may not speak, but my mind is at full capacity. I just play along with the charade. If they want to believe such things of me, then let it be.

It can be ironic here at times; the way they think they are so smart, so sane. Everyone has a piece of insanity within, don't you agree? The patrons here were just born with a little more "obvious" insanity than the rest of the world. If most people owned up to their insanity, maybe the rest of the world would be diagnosed with sanity and we would lock them up for not fitting into our society.

How gracious that would be. Don't you think so, Doctor?

I think of these kinds of things quite often, but I do not share them with others. No, I like the world inside me. It is sacred. No one can invade it. No one can judge it. That is what bothers them around here the most. They do not know what I think or feel. They do not like not knowing. That is why I chose not to communicate in any way with that doctor—because then they would win.

I liked it when Dr. Huxley was here. Although this place is really all I have ever known. I don't really remember much of when I lived outside of here. They would talk in bits and pieces about me. They think that because I do not talk that I also cannot hear. My hearing is very well, thank you.

Dr. Huxley once explained to a nurse, who was most irritated at my lack of speaking, that I had seen things as a small child that I should never have seen. They say words like traumatic, brutal, torture and something about my mother and father. I do not remember such things, but I do have dreams. Dr. Huxley called them night terrors. That's when your nightmares are really bad. They make you feel terror and you can even hit and flay about in your sleep, waking upright in sweat and terrified with your heart beating so fast it feels like it's going to rip through your chest. When Dr. Huxley was here, these bad dreams had eventually went away, but now the night terrors are back and worse than ever.

It is the same dream each time, but the horrific feeling at the end is getting worse. The dream starts where I am swimming deep in an ocean like a fish. I have no need to hold my breath; I am just naturally swimming. The water is warm and feels good, then suddenly the water is ice cold, and an awful feeling overwhelms me. I look behind me and see from afar that a huge shark is darting towards me. I swim as fast as possible, but I feel that the shark is getting closer fast. I look up to the top of the ocean then swim up at an unearthly speed and quickly come to the surface. When my head breaks through the top of the water, I scream for help. From out of nowhere, a man pulls me up and into his small fishing boat. I look up at him and somehow this man is actually me, but as an older man. As I cough out water, the shark jumps up out of the water. The old red haired man that is me, stabs the shark with a spear and throws the shark down into the boat. The shark lays in front of me dead and it appears to be only a couple feet long now. The man chops the shark in half and over a hundred yellow bunnies pop out and jump into the ocean. They all swim away happy. But one yellow bunny will not jump out—it just sits in the boat. I look for the red haired man, but he is gone and I begin to get the chills. The ocean begins to get rocky and I lean over to pick up the soft yellow bunny and it bites my hand with piercing teeth which sends a sharp pain from my hand up through my arm. I start crying and ask the bunny why it did that, but the bunny looks at me blankly. The ocean is stormy and the clouds darken as I sit there and cry uncontrollably. Then, I wake up. Sometimes still crying. Each night the dream gets more and more vivid. I cannot control the dream at all. I am always scared of the shark, and pick up the bunny that bites me, and I always cry endlessly.

I want these dreams to end, though I do not, of course, tell them here of such things. Oh, how much excitement they would gain knowing I suffer in any way. I am most certain they would give me medication to make me sleep even more, to endure these night terrors at a frequency most unbearable. They do not treat us in any humane manner—

we are nothing. They do not even address me by my name; I am simply referred to as vegetable girl.

Dr. Huxley came up with my name, you know. Pepper. I do not remember my birth name, but Dr. Huxley told me when I was a little girl that my bobbed red hair and freckles reminded him of Peppermint Patty. He always read the Peanuts cartoons to me. "There's my little Peppermint Patty," he would say in delight as I showed up for class. I hated that he thought I looked like Peppermint Patty because I thought she looked a lot like a boy, rough and unruly. I thought of myself as a girl who was strong and independent, yet sweet and proper. However, the smile it brought to Dr. Huxley's face made me grit his "There's my little Peppermint Patty." Eventually, and much to my delight, by the time I was ten years old my name shortened to Pepper. Spicy is much more flattering.

What I had appreciated about Dr. Huxley the most was how he respected my desire not to talk and my pretending not to hear. He did not admonish me for that. Instead, he taught me sign language and taught me to write and read. When any staff questioned why he bothered doing so, Dr. Huxley explained that people do not need voices or hearing to communicate, they just need communication tools. He would have me write papers about a book I had read and would give me tests. He would tell me that once I was out of Emerson Rose, I was going to go far with my education, but I knew I was not ever leaving here. This place was all I had ever known.

I had read every book in our library more than once by the time I was fourteen, so Dr. Huxley had me help by being a nurse's aide. I presume it was because I was never a threat to the others and was merely a mute. I was allowed to help with bandaging wounds, taking and writing down blood pressure, and taking temperature. I listened to the nurses ask questions and discuss each diagnosis. I absorbed it all. A couple of the nurses brought me medical manuals, which I read front to back. I would write down questions that they would answer. By the age of seventeen, I was becoming more and more interested in becoming a nurse. Then Dr. Huxley died and in came Dr. Vanodin.

The first thing Dr. Vanodin did was fire all the staff here, including the nurses. I never made mention of my experience and Dr. Huxley, seemingly blessed with a lot of foresight, it seems never documented my nursing advancements in my records. Consequently, Dr. Vanodin came to me saying that my records showed I am an idiot for I had made no progress since my arrival. From then on, I just sat in a chair in front of the recreation room window, staring at the trees.

The orderlies and nurses try to say and do things to make me talk or make noises, but I do not react. They do this to antagonize me into talking, but I just stare out the window. They close the curtains on me at times, so I stare at the curtains. I refuse to let them get any kind of emotion out of me. They do not like that here.

Why do you suppose they feel the need to get something out of me? What does it matter to them? How funny that they have made that so important to them.

In the beginning, Dr. Vanodin tried to get something out of me by burning my hands in hot water. Then he did hydrotherapy, electric therapy, et cetera, et cetera. But, he finally declared me an "incurable mental retard"—at least that's according to the sign I am required to wear around my neck. If I don't wear the sign, I don't get fed. I also do not want to end up behind the walls. I think my diagnosis has saved me from that thus far.

I would like to believe that Dr Vanodin giving up on me was a good thing, but I know about the calm before the storm. They are getting ready to break me, somehow. The beginning treatment is always humiliation and then one day you're just gone…sent to the other side. We are nothing but lab rats to him and his staff.

When Jackie came to me for help, I was on board immediately. Must seem silly to come to a mute girl for help, but Jackie knew I could be important to them. She knew Dr. Huxley and I had conversations with our hands, sign language – silent words. So it is through me that we have created our own language and a way we can all communicate without others knowing. We mostly use only one hand, for that is all Jackie has to use.

Five leads work with Jackie. Each lead is in charge of recruiting different patients and each have a different role. Only the leads know that Sabel is in charge. Only I know that Sabel is not really in charge, but working with someone else above her. I don't know which patient it is, but whoever it is, this person seems to have unlimited access to meet our needs. They use a fist as a symbol to identify this commander of sorts. Sabel chose me to know about the Fist, because if ever caught, she knows they would not be able get me to talk and that I, of course, would carry on the mission at any expense. I only presume that the Fist would know to come to me.

The patients who are involved in the plan have all drawn the letter H with a circle around it somewhere, either on their body or in art pictures. To further communicate and help inspire the mission, these same patients have also manifested a finger sign for H. The H, of course, symbolizes Dr. Huxley.

Sabel's plan involves a total of forty-five patients (including the five leads). Because there is only twelve staff on duty per each shift, we do have the advantage in numbers. Because Dr. Vanodin hires most of his orderlies due to their sleaziness instead of their strength; we also have muscle on our side. Plus, most of the patients here really are crazy. Crazy enough to do whatever it takes to overtake them all.

Four of the leads have been assigned a section of rooms. The patients know who their leads are and not much more. Their orders are to simply follow their lead and fight until the end. They also have been given instructions on how to create and/or find a weapon of some sort, if the need arises.

Walter has given Jackie the layout of the asylum on napkins, piece by piece. From there, a route for the escape has been planned. Walter has access to one set of keys and Sabel is in contact with two others with whom she will also be getting keys. I am not sure who they are. It could even be you, Doctor.

Once out of the asylum, a ferry will be waiting to take us to shore. From there, we will turn Dr. Vanodin and his staff into the authorities and tell them what they have done to us. They must act quickly before he kills all those patients locked up on the other side of the wall.

Dr. Vanodin must pay for what he has done. I do hope they will care enough to punish him and his staff. I hope we are not turned out into the streets or locked back up into the hands of the devil himself.

Well, Dr. Quill, I must end this letter. It will soon be mealtime and once again, they will probably take away my utensils or pour Tabasco all over my food. I will once again portray a picture of unmovable emotion when they try to get something out of me. Sabel has Jackie telling everyone how important it is that we write our stories down and get them to you, but Sabel never explains why doing this is so important. But I know why. It is because if we do not make it out of here, if Dr. Vanodin and his staff win this war, someone has to tell our stories. And it looks like, Dr. Quill, that someone is you.

With warmest regards,

Pepper

7

DILL LIBERATOR

I'm writing you because I know you're involved somehow. Something's going down and I can feel it. I can see it in their eyes. I want to be a part, I want to help them and get out of here, too. They think I'm a crazy old lady, so they don't come to me. They think I'm too crazy to be of help. Pretty bad when crazies think you're crazy. Just because the damn pickles are out to get me, they all stare at me as though I'm a madcap. Even the lettuce and tomatoes are laughing at me. They think it's funny that the other patients call me whacko. But I'm telling you, Dr. Quill…I'm not a loon.

That Dr. V is an asshole, I tell you. He had me locked up in solitude for a month just because I threw away all the pickles then lit the trash on fire. It took me six months to get on kitchen duty to do that. The lettuce and tomatoes weren't laughing then; they were shaking like a tossed salad. Nothing worse than being in solitude. Alone. No sound. No anything. Makes you think you aren't alive. That you are just there in a void of nothing. I didn't like sleeping either, because that just meant bad dreams.

The bad dreams were the worst. Of course, it was always dreams about pickles! The worst dream I can remember was when I was on a playground yelling at a bunch of pickles that were standing around talking, but they wouldn't listen to me. They just kept talking louder and louder. So I walked over and kicked them all. The pickles rolled all over then got up and started chasing me. I ran to the front doors of Emerson Rose, but the doors were locked. I saw Dr. Huxley in the window and he shook his head and wouldn't let me in and then all of a sudden, I turned into a pickle. I screamed and screamed. Then I woke up.

It was beautiful to watch that kitchen trash can on fire…watching the blaze and the pickles as they screamed to their death. I smiled and waved good-bye. I did. A couple of them tried to make a run for it, but I threw them back in. Little dill weeds.

Now they're back and they won't leave me alone. Dr. Huxley made them go away.

"Elora Finkel, the pickles, lettuce and tomatoes are only your enemy if you allow them to be."

I asked him once if he was on the pickles side, if he was a pickle, he looked at me sternly. "Elora, do I look like a pickle?"

I fish eyed him real good then realized he was too nice to be a pickle.

But pickles are everywhere, you know. I couldn't go anywhere without seeing one. When I was eleven years old, my mother dropped me off at the orphanage. That became my new home, but there were pickles there, too. No matter where I go, there are pickles on somebody's plate. If I saw the pickle on the other kids' plates, I would scream and throw their plate. That's how I ended up here.

It doesn't mean I'm a loon just cause pickles talk to me.

Look at that fat lard, Delta. she's the real loon. Going around thinking her looks are movie star-ish, but she's ugly gone criminal. Hell, she'd scare the bumps off a pickle. Stupid cow. At least I can look in the mirror and know what I look like – an old haggard woman! Like that one in the Snow White movie giving her the apple. The pickles have made me age something fierce, I tell ya.

Dr. Huxley knew I wasn't crazy. He did tell me that my words scared these patients. I can't help it if these slow asses can't keep up with my words! One day, I was trying to warn a patient that he had a vicious pickle on his shoulder. The whacky came up to my face, threw his hands in the air, and yelled, "blahity, blahity, blah, blah, buh, buh, blahity!" or something like that. Anyway, he scared the living bagezzers out of me and I slapped him across the face. He stopped yelling and just stared at me while I glared back at his crazy ass.

Dr. Huxley was there all of a sudden, telling the crazy to go to the recreation room, and then he looked at me with scorn.

"He's the crazy one!" I pointed out.

"He was mimicking you, Elora. That's how you sound to others."

"What?" I crossed my arms tight. "I don't sound like that crazy ass."

"Maybe it does not sound that way to you, but it does to them. Do you want the patients to slap you when you do that?"

"If I sound like that crazy ass, then yes. But I don't. So nobody better be slapping me or so help me—"

"Okay, Miss Finkel, why don't we get you over to the recreation room and work on your painting."

It was the most sensible thing the doctor said in that conversation. He told me we would work on my perception of things, but the next day Dr. Huxley was dead. Then that asshole Dr. Dillweed Van-whatever came along, and he's been worse than any damn pickle I've ever met.

Can you tell them, Dr. Quill? Let Sabel and the rest know I'm not crazy. They won't listen to me. Let them know I now have the pickles on our side. The pickles want to help us. They can, you know. The head pickle, Gustaw, he has many great ideas. I keep him in my pocket during the day, under my pillow at night. Gustaw says if we all drink pickle juice, it will give us great strength to defeat Dr. V and his evil people. Tell them I will help. Tell them to drink the pickle juice. Tell them that the pickles will help set us free!

8

NOT SO BELL

May 20, 1978

Dearest Dr. Quill,

   My name is Delta Fay. I will begin by informing you that I do come from the utmost prestigious of upbringings. My father was a prosperous oilman in Texas, and quite influential, you see. Although I never had the pleasure of meeting his acquaintance, my mother told me of his many attributes. After mother gave birth to me in Dallas, we moved to Nevada where he was to join us. His work, however, pervaded his doing so, although he sent mother money often so she never had to work.

   I was fortunate in that my mother was able to be home with me all day. At night, however, she always dressed up real pretty. Mother told me how she had to go to night parties to mingle among the influentials. It was important for mother to attend these parties, you see, for that's what a proper socialite does to secure her future.

"These parties are to make sure my little Southern belle is taken care of well," she would tell me as she patted me on the head.

I always had Sally there at night to watch me. She attended day parties, so it worked quite wonderfully. Sally was real amiable, but not as alluring as my mother was. I believe Sally was much older than mother, but she always claimed they were the same age.

Mother had always called me her Southern belle and said my beauty would make Scarlett O'Hara jealous. Scarlett is the main character in a book called *Gone with the Wind*. Mother began reading it to me when I was real little. That was until I learned to read, then I read the book to her. I loved Scarlett O'Hara. When mother's party dresses were too old for her, she gave them to me to wear. I would dress up in them, put on some of mother's makeup and prance around acting like Miss Scarlett.

> "Oh, Rhett! Please don't go! You can't leave me! Please! I'll never forgive you!"

Sally said I was quite the sight, which meant beautiful.

I never had a Rhett Butler, but mother said I did not need one. She said a real Southern belle needs only her beauty and charm.

When I turned ten years old, mother and I moved to California. She said there were more profitable parties out there. Mother said the sun always shined, and with my beauty, I could have what I wanted because California was the land of opportunity. But it did not turn out that way, Dr. Quill, the sun did not always shine in California.

We had been there no more than a month when mother was arrested for attending a party. She said the police did not like socialite parties. She said it was because they were not allowed to attend, so it made them real jealous. In Nevada, the police could attend the parties, so we never had any trouble. California was real different that way and mother was arrested many times.

Then mother did not return for several days. I was in our studio apartment alone because mother said I no longer needed anyone to look after me and that I had become a very self-sufficient young lady. I was eventually living off the last of the canned soup, as that was all we had left in the cupboard. I had no money to buy groceries, no phone to call anyone. It was so cold…as our heater did not work properly and only one blanket covered the mattress on the floor. I tended to myself by alternately reading the three books I had, *Gone With The Wind*, *Animal Farm*, and *A Street Car Named Desire*.

Then one day there was a knock on the door. I answered it without thinking and without looking through the tiny peephole first. A lady dressed in a two-piece suit stood in the doorway. There was a police officer standing next to her.

"Are you the daughter of Fay Morgan?" the officer asked.

I could feel tears burning the back of my throat. "Where's my mother?" I choked and then burst into tears.

One of the ladies squatted. "Your mother is fine. She is just in trouble and will be gone for a while." The lady grabbed my hand and I snatched it back thinking to myself, *"Will she be gone?"* (quote from GWW)

"Where is my mother?"

"What's your name, honey?" the lady asked.

"Delta Fay." I sobbed.

"That's a beautiful name." She smiled. "Well, Delta, would you like to go with me and get some ice cream?"

I was ever so cold, although I had a blanket around me, but I agreed to go get ice cream because I was also very hungry. The lady took me to dine for lunch at a local café. She explained how I was to go live with a temporary family. She told me it would be some time before I could see my mother again, but the truth of the matter was, Dr. Quill, that I was never to see my mother again.

Within a couple of days, I was forced to reside with the horrific Jones family. They had five heathens for children and were insufferable, bearing no manners at all. I tried to pay them no attention, but sometimes that was not so easy. I would dress up like Scarlett and recite from *Gone with the Wind*. Those other kids were just horrible and would laugh at me, saying I was crazy. Saying I was "Gone to the Bin." The oldest girl, who was seventeen, was the most evil to me. She would say I was so ugly that it was no wonder my mother and father dumped me.

Then one night she was getting ready for a date and I needed to go to the bathroom real bad. She was ratting her hair with a pick and hairspray and I told her nicely I needed to use the ladies' room. She told me I was no lady and I could pee my pants for all she cared. Then she looked at my reflection in the mirror and saw that I had put on makeup.

"Good God." She put the cigarette hanging from her mouth into the sink and then picked up the hairspray can. "Did your mother look a whore as much you do?" She began to laugh as she sprayed her hair. Without her knowing, I picked up the lighter next to the sink, flicked it on, and held it next to the back of her head until it ignited the spray from the can. Her hair blew up in one big Poof. I watched in amazement as the ball of fire quickly swept over her head and onto her face. The girl screamed frantically as she tried to feel for the water faucet, but I kept knocking her hands away. Her screaming became louder and louder... then I heard footsteps running up the stairs so I made a quick escape out the back door.

They found me a couple days later and I was put into a hospital. When the mother came to visit me, my hands were strapped to the sides of the bed.

"Do you," she said and began to cry, "Do you know, you awful little girl, what you have done to my Cindy? Her face… she will never be the same!"

I mumbled softly in response.

Mrs. Jones moved in closer. "What?"

I mumbled softly again.

Irritated, she demanded loudly, "Speak up, you vile child."

I responded softly. "I said…" Then suddenly, loud in her ear, I shouted, "Frankly, my dear, I don't give a damn about that bitch daughter of yours!"

She slapped me across the face and I began to laugh hysterically. She ran out the door, blubbering about my being crazy. Shortly after, I was sent here.

I do have my dear sweet Charlie, though I am unsure of his actual height. When he stands next to my six-foot figure and I look down at him, he seems pretty much like a circus midget. However, when he stands next to others, he clearly is not. His round puffy eyes, round cheeks, and round belly remind one of a cherub. You know those little chubby angel statues you see in gardens? Charlie always beams the most beautiful smile when he sees me. If his heart flutters as wild as his eyes do whenever I'm around, then that young man is truly in love with me.

Charlie calls me his "Belle"—he says it means beauty in French. He is quite intelligible about those sorts of things. Charlie is not much for talking when others are around. When I am the only one in his company, Charlie tells me stories of all of the traveling he has done back when…well, back when before he was here. Charlie goes wherever I go and I do adore his admiration. Though I do declare, I do not have the same feelings for him that he does for me. For that matter, he is truly no Rhett Butler. But he is, well…quite frankly, he is Charlie.

They try to break me here, Dr. Quill. The other day I was in Dr. Franks' office. He sat with his old skinny legs crossed and his beady eyes staring at me over his wire-brimmed glasses. He looked a whole lot like a Deadwood weasel.

"Delta, you are not pretty. In fact you resemble a *wildebeest* that has fallen into a bucket of makeup."

I was not acquainted with what a *wildebeest* looked like, but he had made it clear that it was not something pretty. His comments did not bother me, no sir. The way he was so adamant about making me feel ugly, I knew my beauty bothered him and it gave me the upper hand,

"Why, thank you, Dr. Franks." I smiled. "I am aware my beauty is more than most men can handle."

He pushed his wired glasses to the bridge of his nose, uncrossed his legs, and leaned forward. "I see." He squinted. "So, tell me then, how do you feel about your mother making money from men?"

I will not repeat the rest of his vulgar words, but I will tell you I came off that sofa and put my hands around his throat.

"Never! Never speak of my mother like that!" My fingers gripped tighter and Dr. Franks' face went stark white and his eyes looked like they might pop right out of the sockets. I picked him up, then let go and he dropped back into the chair. I grabbed my shawl off the sofa and looked back at the petrified Dr. Franks.

"Never," I said as I pointed my finger at him and sauntered out the door.

That night, six orderlies and a nurse came to my room.

The nurse gave me a shot that knocked me out and then the orderlies, I suppose, carried me to a room I had never seen before. When I awoke, I was in a large leather chair with a tall back and my hands and feet were tightly strapped. Bright buzzing lamps shined down on me. A doctor I had never seen before came in, he was Chinese or Japanese or something like that. English was definitely not his first language and his manners were worse than that of the Jones family.

There was only one nurse and she stuck something on my head. Next thing I knew, I was being electrocuted or whatever they call such a thing. It was quite awful and tears did find my face in that moment.

The next morning, I awoke in my room a little out of it, but I was fine, really. At lunch, Charlie kept looking at me with eyes that asked, "What happened?"

"I'm fine, Charlie," I said, trying to reassure him as I patted him on the head. He did not seem convinced.

Sabel had Jackie come to me after lunch to ask if I wanted a chance to get out of here. I told her I was fine and where else would I go anyway. Judging by the perplexed look on Jackie's face, I am not sure they had given much thought about where they would go either. Nonetheless, I am not going anywhere and that Sabel needs to watch her ways. Dr. V has many eyes and ears around this place. If Sabel does not be heedful, she will end up like the others, resting in peace amongst the trees behind Emerson Rose with only a number to remember her by.

Well, Dr. Quill, Jackie mentioned that you were requesting letters to record the final weeks before Sabel's plan is executed. For the record, I wanted to assure you that I like my stay here at the Emerson Rose. These doctors can fry me like an egg, but my spirit will always remain strong. I do not support this insane plan of revolution, as it truly seems foiled from the start, but I suppose it will be fine if all goes as planned. On the other hand, I have seen too many fools think themselves clever for they had fools supporting them to think so.

With Distinguished Salutations,

Delta Fay Morgan

9

BURNED

Dear Dr. Quill,

Welcome to the Freak Show, brought to you on behalf of Dr. Vanodin, where we have whackos, both patients and staff alike, for your constant entertainment. Yes, it is the ridiculous, preposterous, idiotic circus of psychos! Step right up!

This place is pathetic. The way these patients talk to themselves, hit themselves, paranoid and scared of everything. There's even this guy here who dresses like a woman. Sad thing is he looks better than the rest of these chicks here. Especially that walrus that looks like she got attacked by some whacked out Avon lady. Now that's a bad case of uglies! Too bad there's no pills to cure that.

Anyway, it's ridiculous here the way these nutcases run around. It's just a building full of people too damn lazy to be normal. Seems like they're just faking this shit. Why not? In this place, they don't have to take care of themselves or be responsible, not even for their crazy actions. It's all bullshit. I watch them, I watch them all. They go about being normal and then a nurse or orderly comes into sight and they go into crazy mode. It's all a scam and everyone here knows it and plays along. Patients pretend to be crazy and take the meds, participate in the groups, saying what everyone wants to hear. The workers here believe it all because they have to. Or guess what, Doc? They're out of a job. But I'm not falling for this bullshit.

I am way the shit more sane than these workers here are, but they don't want to see that. Especially that bitch nurse, Darly. She runs the "happy" group they make me go to or I get zapped in the head. Darly sits there and looks at me with her frog eyes, pointy nose, and prune lip face that I want to just punch; and tells me I need to get in touch with my anger. I told her why don't I smash her fucking head in and let's see how that makes me feel. How that will help me get in touch with my anger. She had me escorted back to my room. She needs to get in touch with the stick up her ass.

Who the fuck is she anyway? She probably had everything handed to her, yet she waddles around with her big ass and thinks she has all the damn answers. Like she knows what it was like for me growing up. She couldn't have handled one day in my house with my father. I barely threaten her and her granny-panties get all in a ruffle. Maybe I should burn her all over with lit cigarettes, threaten to kill her, and then as she is yelling at me to stop, I would tell her, "Don't let it get to you. Get in touch with your anger, Darly."

My father loved to use me as a human ashtray and I'm the one who is put in the fuck'n looney bin. It's bullshit. When I was six years old, my father thought it was real funny to reach out to mc like he was going to give me a hug so that I'd run to his arms, but right when I got within reaching distance, he'd kick me.

"Boys don't hug!" he'd yell. I had already learned not to cry in front of him, because boys do not cry either, ever.

I wasn't the only punching bag; mother had her share, too.

That was until she left him and me, anyway. I ran away

once when I was thirteen. When the cops returned me, my father was so fuck'n pissed for embarrassing him that I ended up with a broken jaw. Which, of course, I claimed I got from falling. Doctors know, but they don't say anything.

After that, I decided to do what I could to stay out of the house and got a job at a gas station. I was a gas attendant and made pretty good tips that I tried to hide under my bed. After my father found out, he made me give him my paychecks. He said it was to help pay the bills, but it mostly went for liquor. I didn't give a shit, though, because I just wanted a reason to stay out of the house.

The guys who worked there were really cool and let me work as late as I wanted. I look back now and think that after seeing my black eyes and burn marks, they most likely knew what was really going on.

Then one night my dad showed up at the gas station. I was playing cards with the guys in the garage when he pulled up and stumbled out of the car. He held up a gas can.

"Hey, gas boy…fill..er up!" he slurred.

I jumped up from my chair and walked over to him. All I wanted to do was get him in the car and get him home.

"Let's go, Pa."

"I said…filler…up, boy!"

I tried to grab him and put him back into the car, but he sucker-punched me and I fell to the ground. The guys jumped up from their chairs.

"Watcha… gonna… do?" he dared them. I jumped up, still dizzy from the sucker punch.

"It's okay, guys, I'm good."

"Ahh…are these your cute little friends who sit around boohooing with you?"

"Yeah, Pa, that's what we do, now let's go."

That's when he passed out in a drunken stupor and fell to the ground. The guys helped me get him in the back of the car. I filled up the gas can and told my boss to take if off my paycheck, then drove my father home.

I was the same height, yet only slightly stocky at the time, so my father's passed out five-eight, two hundred-fifty-pound balding fat ass was too heavy for me to even think about budging. I picked the full gas can up off the floorboard, looked at the disgusting piece of snoring shit and softly closed the car door. I waited for a second to make sure he didn't wake up and when I was sure he was out for the count, I placed the gas can on the hood of the car. I ran into the front door and quickly packed whatever would fit in my backpack. I grabbed his Zippo lighter off the kitchen counter on my way back out and ran back to the car. I poured the contents of the gasoline can onto the hood. I lit the end of a stick laying in the front yard, threw it on the doused car, saw the blaze start, and darted off. I was some yards away when I heard the explosion. I smiled.

I hitched rides until I ended up in the city. I was able to get a job as a gas attendant and live in a roach motel until I made enough money to live in a building one step from being condemned. It had more rats than it had tenants, but it was still better than living on the streets. I could afford food, beer, and getting tattoos.

My first tattoo was a two-inch black heart with red and orange flames around it. I had it tattooed on my right forearm so I could see it every day and relive the warm, pleasant feeling of freedom that filled me when I heard – *Kaboom! Kaboom, kaboom, kaboom!*

Things were good for a couple of years. Then one day there was a loud knock on my door and when I opened it, there stood two cops.

"Mr. Joe Henry?" the fatter cop with a buzz cut asked.

I just looked at him.

"Are you the son of Patrick Henry?"

I pulled the cigarette from behind my ear, put it in my mouth, and then lit it with the Zippo.

"Who wants to know?" I asked.

There was a couple seconds of silence, and then the scrawny cop with curly red hair finally spoke, "Your father. He's been looking for you." I choked on the cigarette and took it out of my mouth, "That sorry son of a bitch who fathered me – he's dead. You've got the wrong guy, buddy."

I put the cigarette back in my mouth then went to close the door, but the fat cop stopped it with his foot.

"You may think he's dead, Mr. Henry, but I can assure you that your father is very much alive."

The other cop barged in and circled behind me. "You're under arrest. You have the right to remain silent…."

I was transported to the jail back home where I found out my father was still alive. It seems when I went to pack my bag, he had gotten out of the car and passed out on the couch. He saw me run past with my backpack and then grab the lighter, but I never saw him. I hadn't checked the back of the car; I'd just assumed he was still in there.

Apparently, when he heard the first explosion, he jumped off the couch and like a dumb ass, ran out front. Part of the blown debris knocked him down and a huge piece of the engine landed on his legs and left him paralyzed from the waist down. Since my father had seen me, it was enough proof to press charges for arson and attempted murder.

At the court hearing, my assigned counsel went for an insanity plea—using my burn scars and medical history and witnesses from a family doctor, neighbors, and former co-workers to prove my father's abuse had pushed me over the edge. So many people had known. I watched my father as they recounted all the abusive events. His face never changed. He never showed any remorse and when his attorney put him on the stand – he denied every single thing.

"Mr. Patrick Henry, have you ever hurt your son?"

He looked down at his legs, trying to draw attention to his paralysis then looked up at his attorney. "No, sir. I have never hurt my son." His chin lifted a bit. "I've always been a good father. He, he was the one who abused me."

I jumped up from my seat. "You lying son of a bitch!" My lawyer went to grab for me, but it was too late. I had already leaped over the table and headed towards the witness stand. The bailiff grabbed me and held me in a giant bear hug, yelling at me to calm down. I tried to pull away, but his grip only tightened, leaving me almost breathless. My father refused to even look at me.

"You god damn lying son of a bitch! I will kill you and next time I won't walk away until I know for sure that you are good and dead."

I was found guilty by reason of insanity and sentenced to five years in an institution. That's how I ended up here. I didn't mind it too much when Dr. Huxley was running this place. He was a cool guy. I asked him one day if I could get a tattoo. He asked why.

"Tattoos are like a roadmap of my life, Dr. H."

I pointed out all the different tats and explained the stories behind them.

"And this one, Doc," I said, pointing to the one on my right calf, "This was the last one I got while I was in jail awaiting my trial."

"I see, Joseph. Hence the broken off arms of Lady Justice."

He looked at me, but I couldn't look him in the eyes, I was afraid he would read my thoughts.

"Well then, Mr. Henry, exactly what kind of tat did you have in mind?"

"I wanted to get a tat of a rose with the letter E on it. You know, as a tribute to being here at Emerson Rose."

"I see." He looked at me funny. "A tribute? Quite frankly, I thought you despised being here."

"I hate where ever I'm at, Doc. This place, though, it's not so bad. At least I have food and shelter. And it is safer being locked up in here with loonies than it is being on the outside where the real crazies are."

He laughed. "I will think about your request."

A week later, a tattoo artist came to my room. I had him tattoo the rose with an overlapping E on my right forearm. Things were good then.

Then came Dr. V and the minute Dr. Van-old-dick showed up, we were all reduced to being cockroaches that scurried under the door to our rooms, hiding in a corner on our backs, legs twitching in the air. The Emerson Rose became the Roach Motel where us roaches check in, but can never check out.

The worst part has been these jerks he brought with him. Especially that god damn little bitchy nurse telling me to calm down and get in touch with my anger. She did get hers once, when that old crazy man bit off a piece of her ear. You would think that stupid bitch would have learned. We all laughed and none of us helped her. But she came to group the next day with a bandaged ear, acting as if nothing happened.

"How's the ear?" I asked, but she said we were here to talk about me, not her.

"Okay, well it made me happy to see your ear bitten off so can we talk about my happy feelings?" I gave her a big smile so she could see I wasn't lying.

"I see." Her frog eyes stared me down. "Why did that make you happy, Mr. Henry?"

"Because you're a bitch and you deserve it." The group shook their heads.

"I see. Do I deserve it the same way you deserved being kicked? Or how about the cigarette burns all over your back and arms? Did your father do that because you deserved it?"

I laughed. "Yes, Nurse Darly, I deserved it. I mean, doesn't every eight-year-old boy deserve it?"

"I do not know every boy, Mr. Henry. I was asking about you, do you feel you deserved it?"

"Yes, and I deserve spankings, too. Would you like to spank me, Nurse Darly?"

The group snickered.

"No, thank you, Mr. Henry. Besides, I have a feeling you would like it."

The group broke out in laughter. I crossed my arms and glared at her. She smiled then ended the group.

I am not sure how she knew my father was the one who scarred me. Lucky guess, probably, but at every group after that, she always loved to say, "So, tell us about your father, Mr. Henry."

"He was an asshole, Nurse Darly, thanks for asking."

Then she continued to push me until I got so pissed that

the orderlies came and hauled me off to my room.

I'm not like these damn crazies. I gave my father what he deserved. That doesn't make me crazy, it makes me a saint or a martyr or some kind of hero that strikes down the bad.

Anyway, there's a group of crazies making plans to escape. So I have decided to join them. I figure with a one-armed chick, the screamless screamer, the big black guy, and a mute girl leading the way that what the hell? Besides, they may just be crazy enough to pull it off.

Joe Henry

10

BIRDS OF A FEATHER

Ha ha, hee hee. I see the pretty blue sky.

Yes, Alex, the skies are pretty.

No, no pretty blue sky

Yes, the sky is pretty with its cotton candy pillow floating above, this is what the birds feast on, you know?

No, no birds. Birds bad. Must die.

No, we will not kill the birds anymore. We must let the birds fly unbound.

No. Pull the wings, rip them off!

We must leave their wings on so they can fly free into the pretty blue sky.

No! No! Rip the wings with teeth.

Watch them fly so pretty, as their wings open through the wind.

No, no watch birds. Must die.

We cannot kill those that fly; we must set them free, Alex.

No, no die. You die!

I will not die. I will live to watch the birds fly.

No, you will die. I will kill you. I will.

You cannot kill me. We both know that will never happen.

No! Will happen will. Hate you!

But I love you.

No, no love - hate!

Hate me if you must, but that will not stop me from loving you.

Yes, yes I will stop you, I will!

Shh, Alex. It is time to sleep now. Think of the days before. The days when mother wore her stunning petticoat dress and would lean down and gently kiss us on the forehead. Her smile shined and the words "I love you, little Arthur" would fill the air like song. That warmed us on the inside, remember? Remember that feeling?

March 2, 1978

Dearest Dr. Quill,

I do apologize for the intrusion, sometimes Alex has a hard time being quiet. He has been very calm for quite some time, but now his anger has been awakened. Alex knows he is not supposed to be angry, but sometimes when he is abruptly disturbed, it makes him irritable and troublesome at best. He has seen a great deal, Alex has. There is much he likes to be most boisterous about, but he must be quiet for no one must know what Alex knows.

You see, Dr. Quill, I met Alex a long time ago. It all began when I was only eight and it was after my mother and father had been tragically killed in an automobile accident. Uncle Ernst was the only surviving relative who would take me in, which meant it was either him or the local orphanage. Living with an uncle I had never met seemed far better than some wretched orphanage waiting for a couple to choose me like a puppy in a pound. So the day after my parents were buried, I was placed on a train with a ticket to Wisconsin.

Uncle Ernst seemed quite nice in the beginning. He had owned a local pet shop that specialized in exotic birds. He was a clever businessman, though, because he also had a front window full of puppies and kitties which, of course, attracted the local kiddies. Uncle Ernst also had a special backroom in the pet store where there were dozens of cages filled with squawking birds from all over the world. He also had a brown plaid couch with a bed pillow. This is where he took me and other children to play his *special* game.

I did not like to play his *special* game. I avoided the store whenever possible. Every chance I got, I would purposely get into trouble at school because banging erasers on the chalkboard meant detention and I was safe for one more day. On the days I was not so fortunate, I learned to vacate mentally from the premises. When it was over, I would run into the cornfield, lie down, look up at the sky, and ask mother and father to make Uncle Ernst stop. Sometimes I felt like I could feel my mother's tears and then it would begin to rain.

There were times I was able to evade the back room because the kiddies would come visit the pet store after school, and alone. I suppose parents felt a pet store was a safe place and that a man like my uncle, who gave so generously to the community, was a most trustworthy man indeed. I always knew which children had paid a visit to the back room whenever they came into the store with their parents. Uncle would want to show the mother or father the specialty birds. The children would begin to cry and scream to their parents that they did not want to go back there. Parents were always agitated at the child's rude behavior and desperately apologized to uncle.

None of us ever said a word about my uncle's secret endeavors. We all knew the price for telling. For Uncle Ernst would pull a kitty from its cage by the neck, dangle it in front of his visitor, and then slowly strangle the baby feline until it was no longer breathing…which taught all of us the importance of being quiet. Very, very, quiet.

NO NO NO birds. Birds bad! Must die! Die die die!

Shh…Alex, it's all right. Go back to sleep. We are safe.

Sorry, Alex does not like me having thoughts of Uncle Ernst. It is very upsetting to him.

I lived with my uncle for one long year before he died of a sudden heart attack. I was placed in a local orphanage and, when asked if I had any other relatives, I swore to them that I had none. I did not want to venture into another relative's house. In fact, I did not want to live in anyone's house. The orphanage suited me just fine.

I lived in the orphanage for three years and no one bothered me there. In fact, nobody paid any attention to me at all and that was just fine by me.

Whenever a couple came to look for a new addition to their family, I always made it a point to act out by cursing, spitting, and throwing tantrums. I did whatever I could to avoid adoption; however, one day a young couple was compelled to adopt me *because* of my behavior. I guess they wanted to save me. So I went home with the Johnsons. All might have been fine, too, if they hadn't had that damn squawking bird.

I despised that foul animal and when it woke me up in the middle of the night with its constant squawking, I wrapped my fingers around its throat and silenced the damn thing. I must say the Johnsons were quite disturbed by the cockatoo's remains in the cage and its decapitated head on the floor. Mr. Johnson quickly packed up my few belongings and took me back to the orphanage. They made me talk to some old senile psychiatrist who immediately had me placed in an institution. That was when I first became acquainted with Alex.

The institution's psychiatrist saw me every day and never quit trying to make me talk about my parents, my uncle, the orphanage, and the incident at the Johnsons. I, of course, refused to talk and would instead just sit there in a comatose state and stare off into the distance.

I would have nightmares about birds breaking out of their cages and pecking at my eyes until I couldn't see anymore. I tried to not fall asleep, slapping and pinching myself to stay awake, but eventually I would fall asleep and then the birds would find me.

Then one day I went into the psychiatrist's office and he had a bird, in a cage next to him.

"What color is my bird, Arthur?"

He wanted me to look at the bird, but I said nothing and refused to look. He described the bird to me, told me its name, and then it squawked. I jumped out of my chair and ran to the corner of the room. I crouched down, put my hands over my ears, and sang, "How much is that doggie in the window?" to tune out that horrendous bird screech.

The pysch doctor bent down next to me and pulled my hands from my ears. "Arthur, speak to me!" he demanded and that was when Alex came out.

"No! No! No!"

"Yes, Arthur."

"No Arthur. I Alex! Make birdie die!"

"I am not going to kill the bird, Alex"

"I kill bird! I kill!"

"No! You will not kill the bird. But I will take it out of here, if you agree to talk to me."

"Make birdie leave! Now! Leave!"

The psychiatrist called for a nurse and had her take the bird away. I went back to my chair and sat with my arms wrapped tightly around my legs. "Are you feeling alright?"

I nodded yes.

"Who are you, Alex?"

I looked the psych in the eyes. "Sir, I have no idea who Alex is, I'm Arthur."

Alex began to visit me in my room when we were alone.

We would talk for hours and we had many of the same interests. We would make fun of the staff at the institution, which always made us laugh so much. We would play games like chess and checkers in the rec room and, at night, I would read him books until we both fell asleep. However, as much as Alex and I enjoyed each other's company, the institution did not see our friendship as appropriate and they tried to take Alex away from me.

They began with ECT and hydrotherapy. Alex despised the cold baths and would cry at night asking why they were trying to take him away. I told Alex no one would ever take him away from me. I knew the only way for both of us to survive was by learning how to keep Alex quiet.

In talk therapy, I pretended to feel well and told them how Alex was gone. I told them what they wanted to hear – I was cured, thanks to their ingenious intervention. Alex and I talked only at night and when there were no ears around. He was very good at being quiet back then and soon the institution let us go free. I was eighteen by then and out on the streets, but I was free. We panhandled for money and stole food sometimes. I had employment as a dishwasher a time or two, but Alex would come out and I would get fired.

One night, we had found a small alleyway between two deserted buildings. An old rusted awning connected the two roofs, but it was enough to keep us dry from the rain. It was a rare find, as there was no one else there. So I found the driest spot and curled up and went to sleep. We must have slept a couple of hours before I was suddenly awakened by someone or something tugging hard on my pant leg. I scrambled to sit up, but my pant leg was being pulled on so hard that could not get my bearings. It was then that I saw the broken shard of metal awning lying on the ground. I grabbed it and flipped myself over on my back. A man with dark greasy hair and a scraggly beard hovered over me. I stabbed him in the eye with the metal shard and he fell to the ground. I kept stabbing him and he started screaming bloody murder. Suddenly a police officer came out of nowhere and grabbed me from behind and drug me off the man. I began to laugh when the officer pulled his gun and pointed it at me…I found it funny that the police were trying to help a criminal. After that, I was the one who wound up being arrested and thrown into a jail cell.

This injustice irritated Alex so bad, he could not remain silent any longer. He yelled all night in the jail and I tried to calm him down, but he was out of control. The next morning I ended up here.

It was wonderful in the beginning, when Dr. Huxley was alive. He knew Alex was my friend and did not try to take him away. Dr. Huxley always treated us as a duo.

"Arthur, would you and Alex like to play a game of chess with me?" he would ask. If Dr. Huxley lost, he would always joke, "Well, Arthur, it was a game of two against one!" That always made Alex and I laugh.

Then Dr. V. came. What horrible people he and Dr. Franks are. Evil, evil I tell you! They despise Alex and are trying to take him away from me. I have tried to quiet Alex and have pretended like he was gone, but it has not worked. They do not ever believe me, and they know to bring in a bird whenever they want Alex to speak to them. It is getting harder to control Alex. They enrage him every chance they get and now they are forcing medicine down my throat. Medicine that is slowly taking me away from Alex.

This is why I have decided to help them—Sabel and the others. So far, I have collected a letter opener, a small glass picture frame, and a candlestick, all of which I keep hidden in my mattress. During my visits with Dr. Franks, I was able to use Alex's outburst as a deterrent in order to sneak each item out…one at a time.

We will escape this caged hell. I will do whatever it takes because I know that they will take Alex away from me forever. I will not have that, no! So I will fight in the battle against them and do all I can to win. Alex is all I have, Dr. Quill. I cannot lose him or I will lose me.

With the most humble of regards,

David House

11

LOVE SICK

May 20, 1978

Dear Dr. Quill ~

The way he brushed back the lock of brown hair always falling across his soft green eyes and his half, turned up smile is what I remember most. He was thirteen and I was twelve, but I knew from the moment I saw him…

Sorry…the memories of him are still difficult.

I suppose I should start from the beginning: My father skipped town right after I was born, forcing my mother to work two jobs to support us both. She waitressed a night shift at one restaurant, followed by a day shift at another. My mother was a short tiny woman who always wore her brown hair in a ponytail that swayed back and forth whenever she walked. I don't really remember the color of her eyes, but I believe they were brown as well. I do remember, however, that she would always bring home leftover food from her day shift. She instructed me to eat only half the meal for supper and to save the other half for the next day's lunch. The only time I really saw my mother was when she would come home exhausted from her day shift, drop the food on the table, and then go straight to bed to get some sleep before her next shift. Sometimes I would get a hello, but most of the time it was only me who said hello.

I had a babysitter up until I was five years old. She was a fat, old grey-haired lady who just sat on the couch eating snack foods that she refused to share, and knitting afghan after afghan. When I was old enough to start school, I was excited and eager to get out of the house. But after the first week, I was wishing I could go back to spending my days with the old fat knitting lady. From day one, I was made fun of at school. Mostly because I had long, unruly blonde hair that spiraled into tiny curls that bounced uncontrollably all over my head. It also didn't help that my clothes were from the local second hand store or that I had to clean them myself in the kitchen sink and wasn't always able to get the stains out or mend what was torn.

The teachers were nice, though, and let me help around the classroom after school. They also took the time after school to help me with English and Arithmetic. I would hang around until the teacher had to go and then I would tread slowly back to my empty home.

When I was ten, my mother sent me to visit my grandparents for the summer. When summer came to an end, and I asked when I would be returning to my mother, my grandma just looked down at the floor and let out a long sigh.

"Well, sweetie," she murmured, fishing for words in her head, "You see…as soon as your mother…well, until she gets her two feet on solid ground…." She looked at me and forced a smile without finishing her sentence.

I was not sure what "two feet on solid ground" meant, but I did know that I was not ever going back to my mother's.

I cried myself to sleep that night, wondering what I had done wrong and why mother didn't want me back. I lay in bed for the next several days, refusing to eat or even bathe. Then on the Saturday before school started, grandma and grandpa came into my room. Grandpa scooped me up out of bed and threw me over his shoulder.

"You are taking a bath, little girl," he declared and tickled me. I tried not to laugh, but I couldn't keep a frown and I broke into a fit of giggles.

Grandpa set me down in front of the bathroom door and Grandma handed me a towel. "You get cleaned up and then we'll take you shopping for a nice new pretty school dress." she said.

She beamed at me and I beamed back.

"I think we should buy her two new dresses!" Grandpa teased.

Grandma gave him one of her "I don't think so" looks.

"Please, grandma, please?" I begged.

"Will it stop you from moping around?"

"Yes! Yes! I promise, no more moping!" I quickly crossed my heart.

On the first day of school, Grandma washed my hair in the kitchen sink, combed through my stubborn blonde curls, and then pulled them back into two tight but pretty braids with ribbons tied to the bottom. I put on one of my new dresses and I felt like a brand new girl. I was sure things would be different at this school and I would finally have friends, but I had not expected Tommy Schumacher.

Tommy and his crew were a year older than I was and they would push, kick, and trip me. They would tell me I was so stupid that my parents didn't even want me. I never cried, though, and I think that's what bothered them the most. If I tried to sit next to any of the other kids at lunch, they would grab their lunch tray and move to another seat. I think most of them didn't want to be between me and Tommy and his crew's line of fire. I would stay safe on the playground by always sitting close to the yard duty teacher and reading a book. I pretty much figured that these bullies would rule my life until I was old enough to buy a car and leave, but that all changed when "he" came into my life.

It was an abnormally hot summer day and just a few days before I would be entering the seventh grade. I had been sitting on the porch reading another *Nancy Drew* book when a moving truck pulled into the driveway next door. The place had been vacant since before I had arrived, so it was exciting to have someone new move to our neighborhood. I tried to appear nonchalant as I looked for any sign of someone that might be my age and that's when Evan suddenly jumped out of the passenger side of the truck. He was a couple of inches taller than I was and I watched as he ran his fingertips across his forehead to brush back the hair that had slid over one eye. I left my seat on the porch and walked over to the white picket fence that divided our houses. He saw me and promptly walked over and introduced himself.

"Hello," he said with a slight nod, "I'm Evan Pierson."

He extended his right hand and I grabbed it and gave it a firm shake.

"Hi, I'm Willow." I looked into his soft green eyes and I could feel my cheeks heat up.

We had agreed, during our brief chat, to walk together on Evan's first day of school. On the way, I gave him a quick overview of the students and then told him about the town and how everybody knows everybody. As we started up the school's front steps, I felt my ponytails being yanked from behind and knew immediately it was Tommy Shumacher. I stumbled backwards and my butt hit the hard cement surface. Tommy and his crew pointed at me and laughed hysterically. Humiliated, I hid my face behind my hands, mortified that Evan was witnessing my torment. All of a sudden, the laughter ended and I could hear Tommy choking out the word "stop." I dropped my hands in surprise and looked up. There Evan was, with Tommy up against the wall in a chokehold. Tommy's feet were dangling in the air and his crew was slowly backing away. Evan looked over at me, then loosened his grip and let Tommy's body slide down the wall until both feet were back on the ground.

"Next time I won't stop," Evan warned as he slowly let go of Tommy's throat. Tommy shook his head dazed and then ran after his crew. Evan extended his hand and pulled me to my feet.

"Are you okay?" His soft green eyes looked watery.

"Yes, yes, thank you."

At first, I thought I was going to burst into tears, but instead I reached over and gave Evan a warm hug. We stood in a tight embrace for what seemed like hours. It was as if neither one of us had ever been hugged before.

From that day on, Evan and I were always together. We walked to school together and he waited for me after each class so he could walk me to the next one. When I look back now, I wonder how that boy ever made it to his own classes on time. We used to sit under the big oak tree in the back of the school and share our lunches. Then we walked home together. After my grandparents went to bed at night, I would crawl out my bedroom window and sneak over to Evan's house. We would lie on the couch and just hold each other until right before we knew his father was due home.

Although we never spoke about it, I knew things were not well in Evan's home. I could hear his father sometimes, screaming at Evan or his brother. I would hear things crash and bang and sometimes Evan had bruises on his face and arms. He always claimed that he had fallen out of bed or down the stairs or he had run into a low hanging shelf. I went along with his stories because I knew he was too full of shame to talk about it. Besides, I didn't want to talk about parents any more than he did.

My grandparents never liked Evan. They did not say as much, but I could tell. I never understood why because Evan's father was the new sheriff in town and everybody thought Sheriff Pierson was admirable. My grandparents may have known how Evan's father treated him and his brother, but if that were the case, I would think they would have been more empathetic. Evan's older brother, Andy, did seem to get himself into a lot of trouble around town, but that was Andy, not Evan. I think, for the most part, my grandparents knew one day Evan would take me away from them.

By the time I was sixteen, I rarely left Evan's side. His father liked having me around because he thought I kept Evan out of trouble. Since his dad was the sheriff, my grandparents had no say in the fact I spent most of my free time at the Pierson's house. My presence also seemed to help keep his dad's temper on an even keel. The one thing I couldn't protect Evan from, however, was the night. Evan and I had agreed that we would not subject ourselves to the temptation of him and I sleeping in the same bed together – we were saving that for marriage. So there were those nights that his dad would hit the bar first and then come stumbling home at three in the morning. The noise was loud enough to wake me up and I would lay there and cry.

When Andy turned eighteen, he packed his bags. He had found a job a few hours away and didn't care that he wouldn't graduate from high school, he just wanted out. Andy told Evan that he was taking him with him because he could not leave Evan alone with their father, but Evan would not leave without me. I could not let Evan live alone with his father either. So we packed our bags and we all left town in the middle of the night.

Things were so good that first year. But then Evan turned eighteen and needed to work to help pay bills. Andy helped Evan get on with the night shift at the cannery where he worked. Ever since we had skipped town, Evan and I had literally spent every second together. Neither of us had been going to school in fear we would be caught and sent back home. However, once Evan began working, he was too tired to spend any time with me and instead slept all day while I sat on the couch and read books from the nearby library. I am not making excuses, Dr. Quill, but that was the beginning of everything going wrong.

Evan and I had still only kissed and held each other at night and though we shared a mattress on the floor, we always stayed fully clothed. I did not know any different nor had I ever wanted to know any different. Evan was gone most nights, but Andy was there every night so we would talk and he would share his day with me. We watched TV, played board games, and shared suppertime together like an old married couple. Andy introduced me to whiskey. It tasted awful at first, but he would mix it with a cherry soda and then I was able to down it. That's how I acquired a taste for it. The best part was, if I drank enough, I would pass out and fall asleep next to Evan. It made the days go by quicker.

Evan was supposed to have the night off on my eighteenth birthday, but he wound up having to fill in for another worker who had called in sick. Evan had no present, no cake, not even a *Happy Birthday* greeting for me. He just grabbed his gear and said he would try to celebrate with me the next night. Without looking at me, he half-heartedly waved goodbye and headed out the door. I grabbed a blanket from the end of the mattress and lay on the couch. I tried to read, but my eyes kept blurring with tears so I gave up and set the book aside. I had just started to doze off when I heard the key in the front door. It swung open and I saw a beautiful birthday cake decorated with pretty, pink roses and Andy was singing, "Happy Birthday to you, Happy Birthday to you."

He put the cake on the kitchen counter along with the whiskey and the six bottles of cherry soda that he had bought just for me.

"C'mon you, let's celebrate!"

I shook my head no and tears ran down my face.

"Hey, birthday girl, there's no cry'n on your special day."

Andy walked over and sat down on the couch next to me.

"Hey, beautiful, no tears."

He wiped my face and then leaned over and kissed me. He kissed me in a way Evan never had and my whole body tingled. His palm held the back of my head as he slowly laid me down on the couch. He lifted my blouse and pushed my bra up, suckling my breasts with his warm lips. I was overwhelmed with a pleasure I had never felt before and I did not want him to stop.

The front door flew open. There stood Evan. With anger like I'd never seen before, he charged towards us. In one quick swoop, he yanked the heavy brass lamp from its resting place next to the couch and slammed it into the back of Andy's head, knocking him to the floor. Evan continued to pound the back of his brother's head with the lamp again and again.

I tried to grab for Evan's arm, crying and begging him for forgiveness, begging him to stop. He finally threw the lamp to the floor and pushed me aside, screaming, "You're a whore!"

He packed his bag and left. I never saw Evan again.

The police came and arrested me for Andy's murder and I pleaded guilty, but they never really believed me. They said that Andy had been hit with a force that my four-foot-eight, ninety-pound body could not have been behind. I stuck to my story, though, so they put me in an institution and told me that they would release me when my memory of who was also in the room that night got better. They must have forgotten about me, though, because I was transferred here a couple of years later.

I have told you my story, Dr. Quill, to help you understand why I must join Sabel and Jackie. Three months ago, Dr. Vanodin started having Delta *zapped* in the head. At first, it did not seem to faze her, but I have to tell you that it was fazing Charlie right from the beginning. Her valiance must have really irritated Dr. V because after a while, they began *zapping* Delta every night and eventually she was just flat out gone. Delta will not come out of her room now. She sits on her bed staring at the wall. Her hair has begun to fall out and she no longer wears fancy dresses or makeup. Charlie just sits on the floor next to her bed and wails.

I deserved losing Evan for what I did to him, but Charlie does not deserve to lose his Delta. I know Dr. Vanodin will continue to zap poor Delta until she is dead and I really believe it's all for his amusement. I will not let this happen to her. I cannot allow them to take her away from Charlie. If there was ever a man who loved a woman, it is Charlie. I will fight for their love in the way I should have fought for mine. True love lasts forever, either from *pure joy* or from *pure pain*. I do not want Charlie to know the kind of *pure pain* that befell me. I have nothing to lose by joining them and there may be a chance I have something to gain. For if I can make it out of here then I can look for Evan. I can find him and tell him the great suffering I have endured. Then he will know my love for him is true and everlasting. Love conquers all and Evan is my all.

Love,

Willow

12

MED SCHOOL

Dear Q -

I am writing as fast as I can. It helps keep my mind off the pain. I need to *not* think of the pain. No. Think of something else. I should tell you things. Yes, things that will take my mind off the pain. It was not always this way. The pain, the meds, shrills in my head. No. But then life, yes, life, schooled me. Lessons were taught. Lessons that can't be taken back. Shit. Here it comes. Break the chalk. Break the chalk. Break the chalk. I can feel it starting at the base of my neck. Damn it! I need my meds. Where is that goddamn orderly? He said if I would let him have his way, he would let me have mine. Asshole. Now it has been three nights of his way and no damn meds for me.

Where the hell is that damn orderly? I keep listening for his keys. I don't hear any keys. I am not putting up with this shit anymore from him. Bastard. If he does not bring my meds this time, I swear to God I will chomp his little pecker right off and teach him who's really in charge around here! I need my meds. The pain, it is coming. It's always the same. The way it slowly crawls up the back of my neck like a swarm of spiders with razor sharp pins for legs. Jab, jab, jab. Prodding into the back of my brain. Then the vomit trying to swim up my throat. The pain gets so intense, I want to grab the back of my scalp and rip it from my head and then tear out my brain. Shit. Shit. Shit. I need my meds. I need them now, before the pain. No pain. No pain.

I just need to keep writing. Writing about things. I can write, yes! I can write about things I learned. Life. Yes, my big fat lesson of pain. I can tell you about that, but if the orderly doesn't get here soon, I am going to teach that asshole a thing or two about pain. I am a professor of pain, Doc. If that worthless little dick bastard thinks he can have control over me like this, he is going to be taught very soon about who is really in control here. He better bring my damn meds soon! Wait. Is he coming? No, no, no! I must write. Yes, keep writing.

Okay. I will tell you things weren't always this way for me. No. Once I had a life of no pain. It was a beautiful life, Doc. There was a time it was just my mother and me and we made the best of that. We had a one-bedroom apartment but mom always had it nicely decorated. When you were inside, you would forget about what was outside. You would forget how next door there where neighbors living in stink, filth, cockroaches. We were always together, her and I. Though I took care of her like I was the mother, we loved each other very much. Then, when I was ten, I came home from school and found my mother hanging by a rope from the beam in the ceiling. I hated her for that. Letting me see her hanging as if she were just some broken light fixture.

But I hated her even more later on for leaving mc with that mother fucker and that poor excuse for a grandma who did nothing to protect me. She just ignored everything. No wonder my mother hung herself.

It was all shit when I lived with them. I tried to run away a dozen times, but the damn cops brought me back. Why the hell do they do that? If I left, why the shit did they bring me back? Dumbasses.

Then when I was thirteen, the eighteen-year-old boy next door introduced me to smoking pot. That was the best day ever for me because I felt nothing and could feel nothing whenever I wanted. I was finally in control of pain free. I did whatever I could do to get pot. I had to have it. Every day. I had to.

By the time I was sixteen, I had grown into a stocky girl— thick muscled and abnormally strong. I was the one the kids at school came to when they wanted somebody's butt kicked. My grandfather had also stopped his bedtime visits when I turned sixteen. He was old and feeble by then. Basically, I could kick his ass, too. which, of course, is exactly what I did. It only took one time because he left me alone after that. I was, however, still subjected to and sickened by his presence and his ever-present repulsive smell. Old people smell. Being high would erase all that, though. The stuff cost, of course, so I ended up stealing from my grandparents to supply my needs. At first, I would sneak just a couple of bills from either grandparent's wallet or from the "secret" can at the top of the closet. Then I finally just said to hell with it and emptied both wallets and took all the money from the can. I still don't feel bad about it. The way I look at it, they owed me.

"You're stealing from us!" my grandfather yelled one day when I got home from school.

"Shut up," I snapped and flipped him off as I headed for my room. He grabbed my arm, but I yanked it from his grasp and looked him straight in the eye. "I will knock you to the moon, old man, if you *ever* touch me again."

He stepped back and I went to my bedroom. I put the *Goats Head Soup* album on my turntable and just as "Dancing With Mr. D" started playing, the door swung open and there the old man stood with a baseball bat in his hand.

Down in the grave yard where we have our tryst, the air smell sweet, the air smell sick…

"Get out! Get out of this house and don't ever come back!" he demanded, holding the bat high in the air.

He never smiles, his mouth merely twists, the breath in my lungs feel clingin and thick, but I know his name, he's called Mr. D...

"That's fine by me!" I snatched my backpack off the bed and, after dumping my schoolbooks on the floor, I shoved what few clothes I had into it as fast as I could.

Will it be poison put in my glass, will it be slow or will it be fast?

"But do know this, old man, I will be back and when I am, I am going to burn this place down with you it." I zipped up the backpack and laughed at his stunned look.

Dancin, dancing so free, dancing Lord, keep your had off

me...

I ripped the arm off the turntable then went towards him like it was a lit torch.

"Get out now!" he yelled as his pale wrinkled face began to turn red and he shook the bat vigorously at me, stumbling nervously backwards.

I dropped the turntable arm and yelled, "Kaboom!"

Still laughing, I walked out the door, sure to keep enough swinging distance between us. I had only gone a couple feet down the hallway before I felt a big thud on the back of my head. I fell to the floor face first. I heard him yell for my grandmother and then tell her to fetch him some rope. I tried to turn over, but he hit me again on the back.

"Stay down. Don't you move," he warned.

My head was pounding, but when I tried to feel the back of my head for blood, he hit me for the third time, only this time it was even harder, and I blacked out.

When I woke up, I was back in my room with my feet and hands bound together. I was hog-tied. I remained locked in my room for what I think was about five days. I had to soil myself repeatedly, but that stopped after the third day…only because they gave me no food or water.

After the fifth day, a couple of pigs showed up. They untied me and as they escorted me out of the house, my grandfather yelled, "She's crazy! She's a loon! Get her out of here and never bring her back!"

I broke loose from the police and ran towards my grandfather. After giving him a swift kick to the groin, I screamed, "Rapist! You goddamn child rapist!"

He fell to his knees and I kicked him in the face again and again until the pigs finally grabbed me and dragged me out the door. I saw my grandma standing in the doorway, watching me ride away in the back seat of the patrol car.

They held me in jail for a few days for "assaulting an elder."

The nice thing was that it was enough time for me to make new drug connections and to find someone who offered me a place to stay when I got out. I told the pigs I had an aunt to stay with and they bought it, but I don't think they gave a shit where I went, as long as it was away.

Once I was out of jail, I did whatever it took to survive— dealt drugs, prostituted, and stole. I also paid visits to my grandparents, much to their horrific dismay.

I would lean on the hood of the car parked in their driveway and smoke, all the while playing with my lighter. As soon as either of them saw me, I would yell, "Kaboom!" and start laughing. Then I would leave because I knew they would call the pigs. Every now and then, the pigs would find me and question my whereabouts, but my new friends always vouched for me and assured the pigs I had been in church with them on that particular day and time.

Drunk and high one night, I paid them a final visit at four in the morning. When I snuck into the house through my old bedroom window, my foot got caught and I fell with a thud to the floor. You would think the noise would have woken them up, but I suppose they didn't hear a thing over my grandfather's snoring. I went to their room, threw open the door and flicked on the light switch.

"Hey, what are you doing?" I screamed loud as I could.

Grandma instantly popped up, pulling the covers close to her chest and looking wide-eyed like a scared mouse. She shoved on grandpa and he finally popped up, too.

"Get the hell out of here!" he yelled.

I laughed. "We'll see about that. Nah, I'm not leaving." I smiled. "Not until after I'm done with the both of you, anyway."

I looked at him and then her. "Do you know what I mean by that?"

Then I pulled out my lighter and lit it.

"What do you think burning flesh smells like? I mean, especially your own. Do you think your skin burning will have its own distinct, nauseating smell?"

My grandfather reached around his back and conducted a desperate search under his pillow, as if trying to catch a mouse. "Watcha gonna do, Grand poppy? Shoot me?"

His searching hand froze.

"Ya' figured it out, huh? I snuck in here this morning while your stupid bitch wife la-la'd in front of the TV folding your underwear. I just walked in through the back door she always leaves open for Max."

Grandma started to cry.

"Oh, and I see you have figured out why little Max is nowhere to be found. Shouldn't have the volume up so loud, Grand momma. It drowns out the quick last yelp a puppy makes when you break its neck.

I smiled. "So what shall we do now? Hmm…"

"Get out! Get the hell out and leave us alone or—"

"Or what, old man?"

All of a sudden, I felt the cold muzzle of a pistol on the back of my neck.

"Freeze."

Like I had a choice at that point. I don't think calling that five-foot pig who arrested me a "piglet" and then asking him where Winnie the Pooh was helped me any that night, but I suppose being in front of the judge really sealed my fate. Especially when I yelled at the cop to lick balls during his testimony, and then laughed and stated that he'd probably like me to lick his piglet's balls instead.

I have been a patron of institutions ever since. To be exact, I have been in two halls of shame. The first were some bullshit, local county crap place where the workers were more fucked up than the patients were. Eventually, however, I was transferred here to Emerson, which was a godsend at first. When Dr. Huxley was here. He was a saint. He was…He's here! He's here! Finally, the goddamn orderly is here! My meds!!!

SHIT SHIT SHIT

I FUCKED UP

He's dead. I don't know what happened. He didn't have the fuckin meds. I have to have them and then he tried and I kicked him to the ground, his keys flew, I ran, ran, and got them, he came after me, but I was stronger and stabbed him in the eye with a key. He fell face first to the floor, I slammed my foot down on his head, I think that broke his neck, his body was just lifeless, but I wasn't taking no chances and I started bashing in his head with my foot harder, harder, blood pooled up, blood is everywhere. I don't know what to do, fuck, I fucked this up, they are going to have a lock down and it's going to mess up the whole plan. Damn it, shit, I hid his body under my covers, but there is blood, blood everywhere, I am going to slip this letter under your door now. Maybe you can tell them Sabel or Jackie, someone, tell them what I did, maybe they can fix it. Shit someone will come looking for that orderly in a few hours, no time – but I do have the keys, I can let everyone out. Shit, I don't know, let them know, tell me what to do, shit, I know. I know I am going to leave this note under the door then I am going to unlock all the doors quietly one by one then we can all be ready. Let them know, Dr. Q, please let them know!!!

13

THE FIST

Dear Dr. Quill,

Due to unforeseen events, I have been informed that we must act as of this moment. Not as we had originally planned. This forces our hand, but we must move immediately. I have attached the letter I wrote and planned on giving you, although I had to cut it short. Thank you for taking on the responsibility of these letters and doing whatever you can do to ensure they get out to the right people, in case we don't.

The Devils Grip will now meet the iron fist.

June 23, 1978

Dear Dr. Quill,

My story is simple: I had a drunk, loser father who took great joy in beating my older brother and me while my mother sat in a corner and stared at the wall. He had already successfully beaten her into oblivion.

I was twelve when I found my mother passed out in a bathtub full of red water. I was home from school and noticed water pouring out from underneath the door. I pushed the door open and there she lay with her head on the edge of the tub, eyes closed, faucet running. I ran out the front door and over to the neighbors. They called the cops and an ambulance.

The police sat with me at the hospital until my dad showed up. One of the police officers tried to explain what had happened to my father, but he didn't want to listen. Instead, he yanked me by the arm and dragged me out the door. On the way home, he screamed at me for going to the neighbors and getting the police and hospital involved. Fortunately, the clanking sound of the Ford truck drowned out most of his words so I just stared straight ahead and tried to block out the image of my mother in the tub.

A week later, my father took me to the mental institution to visit my mother. She was dressed in a white gown and had bandages wrapped all the way around her wrists and up to the crease in her elbow. We sat across the table from her in the recreation room. She never made eye contact and mumbled nonsense when father asked her anything. I was disturbed by the surroundings. People walking around talking to no one, yelling, or hitting themselves. It reminded me of the movie "Night of the Living Dead." After that day, I knew one thing for sure. I would never let myself end up as a mental patient.

Mom came home about a month after that but she was never quite the same. She couldn't carry on a conversation and she mostly sat in front of the TV, even if there was just static. She didn't cook or clean, she either sat or slept. After a couple weeks of playing Mr. "Nice Guy", my father got fed up.

"God damn, woman, get your ass up. You don't get to sit around and not do shit because you think it's cute to cut all over yourself and then abandon us."

She sat in the chair, staring at the TV.

"Did you hear me, you imbecile?" he screamed.

She did not move.

He charged forward and back-handed her along the side of the head. She fell to the floor. She lay there, not moving.

"Get your god damn ass up," he yelled then kicked her in the ribs. She stood up slowly, smoothed the folds of her dress, and then walked into the kitchen. I was sitting at the table, pretending to do my homework. I did not look up, but kept my nose buried in my history book. She pulled out a kitchen drawer and removed something. I snuck a quick glance at her and saw the butcher knife in her hand. I didn't have time to even think about stopping her before she ran back into the living room, but I knew what was about to happen. I jumped out of my chair and rushed out the back door. I ran over to the neighbor's house. I had a feeling my father wasn't going to be around to be pissed off at me again.

By the time the police got there, he was dead. My mother had bludgeoned him, according to the police, twenty-two times. The Coroner's office said the first stab probably killed him instantly. Shortly thereafter, she was put back into the mental hospital and I was sent to live with my grandparents.

My grandfather had been wheelchair-bound and was no better than my father had been. He yelled at my grandmother all the time to "do this and do that" and "to do it now!" Nothing was ever right or good enough. As soon as I turned eighteen and got my high school diploma, I left. I never saw either one of them again.

I took a job as a dishwasher in a run-down restaurant in a town about ninety miles north of my grandparents' place. From there, I went from dishwashing job to dishwashing job until I was finally a good three states away. Eventually, I became a bar-back then a bar everything. I spent more time drinking than cleaning, which also led to a lot of fistfights. Something about the excitement and adrenaline rush of a good fight really got me going. Any man who thought he could push me around would learn real quick that he couldn't. Sometimes even to the point of me putting him in the hospital.

One night while I was hanging out at the bar, I guess I wasn't as drunk as usual, because I blindsided a guy for no reason. Why? Because I could. He hit the floor hard and when his dazed eyes looked up and pleaded for me not to hit him again, I saw my mother's eyes from many years back. I realized then I had become the same monster my father and grandfather had been.

I wanted to stop at that point but, to be honest, I couldn't. I had inherited my father's blue eyes and his mean temper. In an attempt to tame my urge to pummel someone, I began taking jobs as a bouncer. I believed that if I had to knock a guy out, he would have deserved it at least.

Eventually I applied for a position as an orderly at a mental hospital. It was actually Dr. V who made me an offer I couldn't refuse. He had asked around and I was the guy who was well known for not caring and would take a guy down just for the hell of it. The money was almost three times the amount I was making as a bouncer and I didn't think I would have a problem with taking loonies down, but I did. Right from the beginning, all I could see was my mother. I was going to leave, but then I realized could be the guy who did the takedowns differently. The other orderlies were violent, much as I had been in my bar fighting days. Eventually, I became known as the takedown king and the other orderlies called on me – less work for them.

What I didn't know about this place, at first, was the other side. The other side of the wall where the patients are treated like lab rats. Worse than lab rats. I only went on that side once. Never again.   All I could think about was what if my mother had been electrocuted, beaten, had drugs shoved down her throat, followed by being thrown into a 6x6 cell with little or no food and water. It was as if these patients were not even human.   I was going to leave at that point but I had nowhere to go. Though, I had made up my mind that I was not going to be a part of this butchery. Then you came to me, Dr. Q, about Sabel and her plan. I knew then I had to do whatever it took to help them. So I stayed. Now I will be a part of butchery, just not of the patients. Maybe in some way it will avenge my mother's suffering. Maybe it will avenge mine.

Harrison

DOCTOR'S FINAL NOTE

DR. QUILL

July 4, 1978

I came to the Emerson Rose Asylum in the winter of 1950. At the time, Dr. Huxley was in charge and busy setting forth new conceptual therapeutic techniques that would help the patient evolve into a functional citizen who could reside within society. I was awestruck by what I had heard about him from fellow colleges and coming to Emerson to work with him became my only obsession.

The Emerson Rose Asylum had been originally founded by an influential group of wealthy families who needed a safe haven for their mentally ill family members. It had been a small institution in the beginning, with the capacity to house only fifty patients. When Dr. Huxley first accepted directorship of Emerson Rose, there had only been forty-three patients but, in just a couple of years, he had whittled it down to twenty-nine. Meaning he was able to send fourteen patients back home permanently. His goal, he would say in jest, was to put himself out of business.

Dr. Huxley figured if he could come up with an effective way for families to work with their mentally ill family members, then he had succeeded in living his life fully.

"Mind you, Dr. Quill," he had told me once and only once, "There will always be those who will have to remain institutionalized and will need a lifetime of care, because *it is what it is*." His face saddened, but then he quickly diverted his attention to another subject.

"Today, I believe, will be the day I beat you in chess, Dr. Quill."

Whether his game playing was intentional or sincere, he never did beat me at a game of chess.

Dr. Huxley called the asylum patients *patrons* because he saw the patients as people. His philosophy was that the patrons of Emerson were here to receive schooling in socialization and would be able to return to the world as a happy and productive citizen. The first part of his treatment plan was for the patient to accept that they had a mental illness. He then worked with the mental illness, not to "cure" it, therefore, he did not treat the patron as if he or she had some kind of plague. The idea was to work *with* the illness not against it. If someone is blind, one doesn't work with them by instilling delusions of their someday regaining their sight; one helps them learn how to interact with the seeing world. Dr. Huxley approached each of their illnesses on an individual basis. He believed and saw most of his patrons as borderline sane. Mind you, though, if the behavioral issue was uncontrollable or too psychotic, where the patron could cause harm to himself or others, then medications and other psychotherapy treatments were utilized. He was a visionary, not a fool.

"They have been treated like loonies for so long, Dr. Quill, that they have come to believe it. When others pointed out to these patrons that their thoughts and behaviors were not like everyone else's, they were also leading them to believe that they were outcasts or loonies. Who defines normal, Dr. Quill? And what makes any human an expert on such things? If we could actually read each other's thoughts, we would see how we all have a little Mad Hatter running around in our head."

He was right and I must admit that I was no exception.

Dr. Huxley's staff taught the Emerson "school" approach. From the orderlies to the nurses, they were here to school the patrons on social skills and the rights and wrongs of social behaviors. Another important factor in Dr. Huxley's philosophy was that Emerson was never to be called an asylum. However, it was never called a school, for that would have been mockery. It was simply called Emerson Rose.

"If, after the therapy and meds, they get their heads on straight and they are still not socially accepted, what would have been the point of the therapy and meds?" Dr. Huxley reminded his staff regularly.

Any staff that could not grasp or accept this philosophy would be asked to leave. Whenever Dr. Huxley let a staff member go, he would remind the others, "One bad apple rots a whole orchard of trees. We are here to be fruitful."

For the most part, Emerson Rose was a kind of haven. It had been decorated with fine art and the internal architecture was fit for a king's palace. The rooms were painted and trimmed with warm soft colors.

"No white walls in our house," Dr. Huxley said as he gave me a tour after I first arrived

The patrons were allowed to decorate their rooms with personal items, as long as they could not use them to hurt themselves or others. Most of the rooms, however, tended to be decorated with pillows and afghans the patrons had made during *Domestic Skills* time. Only those who could safely handle a needle were allowed to sew these items. Those who could not, received them as gifts from the sewing group.

The patrons were also allowed three 4X6 picture frames with no glass. Most of them did not have actual photographs, so they would draw pictures of those they loved during *Art Time*. Only pictures that made you smile were allowed and, more often than not, they depicted the patrons themselves or comic book heroes. Some of them drew Dr. Huxley.

It never felt like we were locked up, even though we were.

Dr. Huxley had made light of the locked doors by saying, "The locks on the doors are to keep you safe from those on the outside."

Dr. Huxley lived at the asylum as well; however, I do not know exactly where his sleeping quarters were. I do know he was always here. If the staff joked to him about taking a vacation, he would jest, "To me, this is a vacation, and it is my home…so I guess you could say this is my vacation home." His warm smile reflected his sincerity.

Our meal times, whether breakfast, lunch, or supper, were called "Family Gatherings." We were asked to be punctual and proper manners were a must. Napkins went on laps, food was eaten with utensils, and only proper dinner conversation was allowed. When a patron did not follow these simple requests, they were excused by an orderly and escorted back to their room. As a result, they would miss having dessert, which was punishment enough for any patron as everyone always looked forward to dessert.

When patrons demonstrated uncontrollable behavior, such as hitting themselves, the staff was trained to handle it in a calm and soothing manner. The behavior would be brought to the patron's attention and they were asked to stop. If they could not stop, the patron had to be excused from the setting and go to their room. Most patrons learned quickly that uncontrollable impulses needed to be acted out in their own rooms. Dr. Huxley felt it was important to give them something they could control, such as leaving the situation.

There were a certain percentage of patrons that Dr. Huxley knew would never leave the Emerson Rose—those with violent behavior and a continual need for sedation. However, Dr. Huxley treated all patrons as though they would be able to leave one day.

"Every patron must have a goal and a purpose or they will feel like they have nothing to live for. We are all here for some reason or another, even if the reason is not apparent or obvious. A honeybee that lands on a flower has its reason for being there, as do we for being here. A flower is not told to grow, it just does. We are here for the patrons. We are their gardeners."

When I first came to Emerson, I had wanted to check in so I could check out. I had thought Dr. Huxley would be understanding and would allow me to hibernate in my room for the rest of my days. However, that thought only lasted one day, for he seemed to need my professional advice on all sorts of matters. Looking back, I realize he had the answers all along; he was merely helping me create my "something."

I became a psychiatrist at twenty-eight—a very young age to come into that profession, and my colleagues initially turned their noses at me. I continued, though, and had a prosperous practice. I mostly treated young wealthy wives with depression symptoms. I suppose my youth was a draw for them. Nonetheless, it gave me the opportunity to specialize and make even more money.

My father had been a surgeon and my becoming a "quack," as he called it, was nothing short of disappointment to him. He acknowledged my quack status on a constant basis. My father's shining glory was my younger brother, John, but I was not jealous. My brother was the type of young man that everyone loved. John was attractive, intelligent, and his humble nature was probably his most alluring trait. His glow lit up every room he walked into.

John, of course, had become a surgeon just as our father had done. John knew how to keep all of us in good standing, though. He was the mediator between my father and me and with regards to my quack practice. John always came to my defense. Kind of ironic, I suppose, now that I think of how things turned out in the end.

My brother, in the prime of his life, was in a horrendous car accident. He had swerved for some reason we will never know, but it hadn't kept his vehicle from slamming into a building. His fiancé was thrown out the passenger side door. John jumped out of the car, blood gushing from the cut on his head and scooped her up in his arms. He held her closely and sobbed uncontrollably as she took her last breath. John blacked out shortly thereafter and he never fully recovered, mentally.

After his fiancé's death, my brother became numb and out of sorts. Depression conquered him first and then it took over my father as he watched John slowly deteriorate. Mother finally came and begged for my help. It just so happened that I was in the midst of learning the latest techniques of a lobotomy and it was being taught by the master himself. At the time, this technique seemingly had extensive success in therapeutic cures—psychosurgery that cut the connection to and from the prefrontal cortex of the brain. It was being highly recommended by the top psychiatrists.

I was young, naïve, egotistical and believed I could play God – I lost.

My mother was against trying this newest method, but I convinced her I was an angel swooping down to save her from this hell. Instead, I became her Satan. John was supportive of the procedure and he would let no one except me perform the procedure. I was not authorized nor licensed to do so, but I did.

I did not attend my father's funeral. How could the psychiatrist son of the man who committed suicide show up for such a thing? I'm sure my mother was there, pushing the wheelchair of my vegetable brother across the cemetery lawn.

Dr. Huxley never asked why I had chosen to check myself into the Emerson Rose. Maybe he already knew through some his colleagues or maybe it did not matter to him. Either way, I was here to stay.

Dr. Huxley treated me as though I were his assistant. Even when I was locked in my room at night, I had always felt like a part of the medical staff and not a patient of Emerson Rose.

Then in the middle of the night on June 6, 1976, Dr. Huxley died of a sudden heart attack. The next morning, as we all rolled out of bed, something awful was in the air. Something was not right. It felt cold, empty. By breakfast, we all knew of his death and the pain of his loss screamed throughout Emerson.

Two weeks after Dr. Huxley's death, Dr. Vanodin took over and he quickly ripped out the soul of this place. Our haven soon turned into the darkest realms of hell.

I am cutting my letter short now, as I have explained why we are writing these letters to you. The patients are determined to overtake Dr. V and his staff. Conviction and faith can be a powerful weapon, but in reality, I am fearful they will lose. However, I consider this an act of valor as they are fighting for themselves and the humane treatment of others. Doing nothing would have been worse than losing. In their doing, they will have at least one victorious battle. This is something no treatment in the world could have ever given them - a purpose.

Epilogue

My name is Cattarina Russell and I am the one who found these letters embedded in a mattress before the Emerson Rose Asylum was torn down. I had thought that this would be the end, the only thing left of the patients, staff, asylum, but I was wrong. These letters documented the last days, but the outcome had not been known and it seemed that the mystery would forever be unresolved. However, these letters were only the beginning, and much to my surprise, they would not be the final *Letters from the Looney Bin*.